Glitter in the Air

The Evolution of P!NK

Laura Shenton

Glitter in the Air

The Evolution of P!NK

Laura Shenton

WP
WYMER
PUBLISHING
Bedford, England

First published in 2025 by Wymer Publishing, Bedford, England
www.wymerpublishing.co.uk Tel: 01234 326691
Wymer Publishing is a trading name of Wymer (UK) Ltd.

Copyright © 2025 Laura Shenton / Wymer Publishing.

Print edition (fully illustrated): **ISBN: 978-1-915246-73-8**

Edited by Jerry Bloom.

The Author hereby asserts his rights to be identified
as the author of this work in accordance with sections
77 to 78 of the Copyright, Designs & Patents Act 1988.

All rights reserved. No part of this publication may be
reproduced or transmitted in any form or by any means,
electronic or mechanical, including photocopying, or any
information storage and retrieval system, without written
permission from the publisher.

This publication is sold subject to the condition that it shall not,
by way of trade or otherwise, be lent, re-sold, hired out or
otherwise circulated without the publisher's prior consent in any
form of binding or cover other than that in which it is published
and without a similar condition including this condition
being imposed on the subsequent purchaser.

Printed and bound in Great Britain by
CMP, Dorset.

A catalogue record for this book is available from the British Library.

eBook formatting by Lin White at Coinlea Services.
Typeset/Design by Andy Bishop / Tusseheia Creative
Front cover photo: Stuart Boulton / Alamy Stock Photo.
Cover design: Tusseheia Creative.

CONTENTS

Preface	7
Chapter One Who's The New Girl?	11
Chapter Two Hey Sister, Go Sister	23
Chapter Three The Second Impression	27
Chapter Four A Party In Full Swing	39
Chapter Five Feel Good, Real Good	43
Chapter Six Emotionally Invested	51
Chapter Seven Still A Rock Star	59
Chapter Eight An All-Star Line-Up	69
Chapter Nine A Pleasant Diversion	85
Chapter Ten About Us	91
Chapter Eleven Hustle	105
Chapter Twelve Dance Again	113
Chapter Thirteen A Woman of Integrity	123
Chapter Fourteen A Legacy Created, A Bright Future Ahead	131
Discography	137
Gigography	155
About The Author	172

PREFACE

Pink – whose real name is Alecia Beth Moore, born 8th September 1979 in Doylestown, Pennsylvania, USA to emergency room nurse Judith Moore (née Kugel) and insurance salesman James Moore – has captivated audiences for over two decades with her unique blend of rebellious rock anthems, pop hooks, and powerful ballads. What sets Pink apart from many other female pop stars is her unapologetic authenticity, which has helped her connect with a broad spectrum of fans on a deeply personal level.

Pink's personality shines through her music and public appearances. She's known for being bold, candid, and down-to-earth, qualities that resonate with fans tired of the overly polished personas often seen in pop music culture. Her fearlessness in sharing personal stories of struggle, love, and resilience often succeeds to create an immediate sense of intimacy with her audience.

Pink's willingness to address personal issues, such as body image, relationships, and mental health, aligns with a broader cultural shift towards openness and vulnerability. This transparency creates a space where fans feel seen and understood, encouraging them to embrace their own flaws and complexities.

Carving out a unique space in pop music with her in-yer-face attitude, Pink's early hits, like 'Get The Party Started' and 'Just Like A Pill', showcase a defiant edge that has drawn comparisons to punk and rock. This rebellious streak has positioned her as an empowering figure for women who challenge societal norms. Pink's feminist perspective, evident in songs such as 'Stupid Girls' and 'U + Ur Hand', critiques the objectification of women and encourages self-respect. These themes resonate in a world where gender roles are constantly evolving, and where women are seeking role models who reflect their desire for independence and self-assertion.

Pink's musical versatility has allowed her to remain relevant across generations. She can belt out powerhouse ballads like 'Who Knew' and 'Just Give Me A Reason' while also rocking out with high-energy hits. Her live performances, featuring aerial acrobatics and intense stagecraft, offer a spectacle that transcends a traditional and more typical approach to pop concerts, appealing to a diverse audience. This adaptability demonstrates her willingness to evolve as an artist, something that fans appreciate in a culture that often values novelty and innovation.

Beyond the music, Pink's advocacy for various social causes, including LGBTQ+ rights and anti-bullying initiatives, further cements her role as a positive force in the industry. She uses her platform to encourage acceptance and inclusivity, aligning with a generation of fans who value social justice and equality. Pink's commitment to being a good role model for her own children, while also advocating for women's rights and social justice, resonates with fans who share similar values.

The most recent expansive biography on Pink – *Split Personality: The Story Of Pink* by Paul Lester, published by Omnibus Press in 2013 – provides an intriguing glimpse into the early stages of Pink's career, tracing her journey from rebellious teenager to global superstar.

Now, by 2025, with a cascade of achievements and life changes that have further cemented her status as a cultural icon, Pink's output and influence has increased by leaps and bounds. Given this evolution, an updated biography is not only justified, but essential for capturing the full scope of Pink's remarkable journey so far.

Since 2013, Pink's career has had a meteoric rise, characterised by chart-topping albums, sold-out world tours, and prestigious accolades. Albums like *The Truth About Love* (released in 2013 but flying high from thereon) and *Beautiful Trauma* dominated the charts, spawning hit singles and resonating with millions of fans.

Her 2017 album, *Beautiful Trauma*, achieved double platinum status in the United States, with its lead single 'What About Us' becoming an anthem for social justice and resilience. This biography provides a comprehensive view of how Pink's music has evolved, incorporating her innovative stagecraft and the empowerment themes that have made her a role model for millions.

Beyond her musical accomplishments, Pink's personal growth and advocacy work have been profound since 2013. She has openly discussed her experiences with motherhood, marriage, and mental health, offering a candid glimpse into her life. These revelations have inspired countless fans and contributed to ongoing conversations about mental health and the challenges of balancing personal and professional responsibilities.

Pink's advocacy for LGBTQ+ rights and other social issues has also grown in prominence, making her an important voice for equality and inclusivity. A more current biography provides an imperative opportunity to delve into these personal and societal changes, shedding light on the person behind the star and the impact she has had on her community and the world at large.

The last decade has been pivotal for Pink, with significant milestones in both her professional career and personal life. The purpose of this biography is to bridge the gap in our understanding of one of pop culture's most enduring icons. As Pink continues to evolve, break barriers, and inspire, it is hoped that this biography will serve as a crucial document, providing a detailed account of her journey, her impact, and her lasting legacy in music and beyond.

In the interest of transparency, as author of this book, I have no affiliation with Pink or with anyone else mentioned within. It is very much a passion project, but one where I hope that as author and reader, we can go on a worthwhile journey together, celebrating Pink's role as a trailblazer, and exploring her profound influence.

Glitter in the Air - *The Evolution of Pink*

CHAPTER ONE
WHO'S THE NEW GIRL?

The late 1990s was a vibrant era for popular music in both the UK and the US, marked by a fusion of diverse genres and a rapid transformation of the music industry. This period was characterised by the dominance of youth-driven pop culture, the rise of manufactured bands, the revival of girl power, the expansion of music television, and the booming popularity of music talent-search game shows.

With teenagers and young adults dominating the music scene, the landscape of pop music was fuelled by a new generation of artists and bands that catered to the tastes and sensibilities of this demographic. The UK and the US saw a surge in pop acts like the Spice Girls, Backstreet Boys, NSYNC, and Britney Spears, who brought a vibrant and youthful energy to the forefront of the music industry.

This era was notable for the emergence of manufactured bands – groups created by producers and record labels with the express purpose of achieving commercial success. The concept of creating bands to fit a specific image was not new, but the late 1990s saw this approach taken to new heights. In the UK, the Spice Girls had epitomised this trend, becoming a cultural phenomenon. In the US, boy bands like Backstreet Boys and NSYNC dominated the charts, drawing in massive fan bases. These bands were often composed of carefully selected members, each chosen for their unique appeal, whilst marketing strategies were meticulously crafted to attract a large audience.

Whether in contrast or in parallel with the concept of a band being manufactured, the late 1990s was a pivotal time for gender dynamics in popular music. With their bold and often all-encompassing message of girl power, the Spice Girls had become a symbol of female empowerment. They encouraged young women to embrace their individuality and assert their voices in a male-dominated space. This movement had a profound impact on the music scene, inspiring a wave of female artists who followed in their footsteps, including Britney Spears, Christina Aguilera, and Destiny's Child. These artists challenged traditional gender roles and celebrated femininity in a way that resonated with fans across the globe.

MTV, VH1, and other music-focused channels had fast become the primary platforms for discovering new music and following the latest trends. Music videos became a key promotional tool, with artists using visual storytelling to enhance their songs' appeal. This visual emphasis contributed to the rise of pop idols who could captivate audiences not just with their music, but also with their charisma and style. Shows like *Total Request Live* (TRL) in the US and *Top Of The Pops* in the UK served as cultural touchstones, where fans could see their favourite artists and stay updated on the latest hits.

As part of the wider acknowledgment of how popular music artists were, to an extent, a manufactured product, there was a wide emergence of music talent-search game shows, a trend that would grow significantly in the following decade. Shows like *Popstars* in the UK, which aired in early 2001, laid the groundwork for the reality TV format in which aspiring singers competed for a chance at stardom. This format revolutionised the music industry, offering ordinary people a pathway to fame and fortune. It also introduced a new level of audience engagement, as viewers could participate in the selection process and follow the contestants' journeys from auditions to fame.

While pop and manufactured bands were dominant, the late 1990s was also a time of considerable musical diversity. Alternative rock and grunge, which had flourished in the early 1990s thanks to Nirvana, continued to influence the music scene. Bands like Radiohead, Pearl Jam, and Foo Fighters maintained a strong presence, appealing to fans seeking a rawer, edgier sound. Hip-hop and rap also gained traction, with artists like Tupac Shakur, The Notorious B.I.G., and Eminem becoming cultural icons.

This musical diversity underscored the complexity of late 1990s pop music, where various genres co-existed and influenced one another.

When Pink began her music career, she was entering a pop landscape dominated by highly polished, carefully manufactured acts. The boy bands and girl groups that ruled the charts were known for their choreographed dance moves, clean-cut images, and love-centric lyrics. In an industry that often valued image over substance, any new artist would need to think carefully about how to navigate the complex game of the music industry.

In 1995, Pink, along with two other teenage girls, Sharon Flanagan and Chrissy Conway, had formed an R&B group named Choice. They recorded a song called 'Key To My Heart' and sent a copy to LaFace Records in Atlanta, Georgia. L.A. Reid, who was associated with the label, heard the song and invited the group to Atlanta to perform live. After watching them perform, he decided to sign them to a recording contract with LaFace Records.

Choice moved to Atlanta, where the label's headquarters was located at the time, to work on recording an album. Although the album was never commercially released, 'Key To My Heart' was included on the soundtrack for the 1996 film *Kazaam*. At a Christmas party, L.A. Reid gave Pink an ultimatum: "go solo or go home." As a result, Choice disbanded in 1998.

After the break-up of Choice, Pink signed a solo recording contract with LaFace Records and began collaborating with producers like Babyface, Kandi Burruss, and Tricky Stewart to work on her debut album.

With recording sessions for the album taking place at Unique Recording Studios, New York City, *Can't Take Me Home* was produced by Kevin "She'kspere" Briggs, Babyface, Kandi Burruss, Terence "Tramp Baby" Abney, Daryl Simmons, and Tricky. Pink also has songwriting credits on seven of the album's thirteen tracks. The record was overseen by executive producer L.A. Reid, and its lyrics mainly focus on themes of relationships.

A dance-pop and R&B album, *Can't Take Me Home* has been compared to TLC's 1999 album, *FanMail*. This similarity is partly due to the shared team of producers and L.A. Reid serving as the executive producer for both albums.

The opening track, 'Split Personality', is like a sudden burst of energy, designed to grab attention and set the tone for the rest of the record. From the very first notes, the track immediately pulls listeners into Pink's world, revealing the edgy, rebellious, and unapologetic persona that would become her trademark. It's a bold statement that commands attention, challenging expectations and announcing her arrival.

The intensity of the track is palpable, with a rhythm that drives forward, creating a sense of urgency and excitement. The lyrics are equally bold, delving into themes of inner conflict and personal struggles. Pink's raw and emotive delivery reflects a vulnerability that feels genuine and relatable. As she sings about the complexities of identity and the contradictions within herself, she challenges listeners to explore their own dualities. This lyrical depth is commanding in how it diverges from the often superficial themes of contemporary pop songs.

What makes 'Split Personality' so stark is its defiant energy. Pink's voice has a rawness and grit that cuts through the production, creating a sense of drama that is impossible to ignore. The driving beat and dynamic instrumentation add to this effect, building a compelling atmosphere that keeps listeners engaged from start to finish. The combination of raw emotion and powerful instrumentation makes this opening track a compelling introduction to Pink's unique style.

It could be considered that 'Split Personality' provides an early glimpse into the direction Pink would take throughout her career. The defiant energy, raw vulnerability, and willingness to tackle challenging themes would become hallmarks of her music.

This opening track captures the essence of Pink's artistic identity, offering a bold introduction that leaves a lasting impression on listeners. It establishes the rebellious and authentic persona that would, to an extent, define Pink's career, making it clear from the outset that she was not just another pop star, but a force to be reckoned with.

'Let Me Let You Know' offers listeners a captivating glimpse into Pink's vocal range and dexterity. What makes this song particularly noteworthy is how Pink channels a vocal style reminiscent of Mariah Carey's elaborate techniques. Through intricate runs, precise control, and an impressive range, Pink showcases her vocal prowess, demonstrating that she is much more than just a pop icon in the making – she's a powerhouse vocalist with a style that commands attention.

In 'Let Me Let You Know', Pink's voice glides effortlessly through a series of intricate runs and melismatic phrases. These vocal techniques require exceptional skill, as they involve navigating complex sequences of notes with precision and fluidity. Pink's ability to execute these elaborate runs without losing clarity or emotional impact is a testament to her vocal talent.

One of the hallmarks of Mariah Carey's vocal style is her capacity to convey deep emotion through complex vocal arrangements. In 'Let Me Let You Know', Pink brings a similar level of emotional expression to her performance. Her voice moves seamlessly from smooth, soulful passages to more powerful, dynamic moments, demonstrating remarkable control over her vocal instrument. This blend of emotional depth and technical precision creates a captivating listening experience, drawing listeners into the song's narrative.

Pink's vocal range in 'Let Me Let You Know' traverses a wide spectrum of notes, hitting high points with ease while also maintaining a rich, resonant quality in the lower registers. This dynamic range adds depth and complexity to the song, allowing Pink to explore a broad array of vocal textures. The way she shifts between different registers with confidence and agility highlights her versatility as a vocalist.

'There You Go', the lead single from *Can't Take Me Home*, quickly became a hit, not just for its infectious beat and catchy chorus, but also for its theme of female empowerment and independence. Upon its release, the song drew comparisons to popular tracks by Destiny's Child and TLC – specifically, 'Bills, Bills, Bills' and 'No Scrubs' respectively – due to its bold stance on relationships and the assertion of women's autonomy. These themes are also echoed in another track from *Can't Take Me Home* – 'Most Girls', which serves to reinforce Pink's message of strength and self-reliance.

'There You Go' tells the story of a woman who has moved on from a toxic relationship, firmly rejecting any attempt by her ex to rekindle the romance. The song's lyrics are direct and uncompromising, with Pink delivering lines that reflect a sense of self-worth and confidence. This attitude is reminiscent of Destiny's Child's 'Bills, Bills, Bills' in how it addresses a partner's failure to contribute financially, and TLC's 'No Scrubs' in how it dismisses men who bring nothing of value to a relationship. Like these songs, 'There You Go' captures the spirit of female independence and empowerment that was gaining momentum in the late 1990s and early 2000s.

Pink's delivery in 'There You Go' is characterised by a blend of sass and defiance, reinforcing the song's message of empowerment. She doesn't shy away from telling it like it is, using a tone that leaves no room for ambiguity. This assertiveness aligns with the broader trend of female artists asserting their independence and challenging traditional gender roles in relationships. Pink's approach resonates with audiences who appreciate strong female voices that aren't afraid to speak out and set boundaries.

'There You Go' was released as the lead single on 18th January 2000. The song received positive reviews from music critics, who described it as "edgy." It made its first appearance on the Billboard Hot 100 chart on 4th March, at number twenty-five. Six weeks later, it reached its peak position at number seven. The single also achieved other notable chart positions, peaking at number two on the Dance/Club Songs and the Pop Songs charts, and number four on the Rhythmic radio chart. The Recording Industry Association of America (RIAA) awarded it a Gold certification for 500,000 copies shipped in the US.

Beyond the US, 'There You Go' entered the top ten in the charts of eight additional countries. It reached the second spot in Australia, where it was certified Platinum by the Australian Recording Industry Association (ARIA) for shipping 70,000 copies. It also received Platinum certification in the UK and Gold certification in New Zealand.

The music video for 'There You Go' was directed by Dave Meyers and first aired on *The Box* in late November 1999. It depicts her getting revenge on her cheating boyfriend. The visuals were nominated for an MTV Video Music Award for Best New Artist. Much like the majority of her work on *Can't Take Me*

Home, 'There You Go' draws heavily from Pink's experience of a difficult relationship and her accompanying mindset.

In 2002, she explained: "When I wrote that, I was really angry at someone I'm probably still angry with. I don't write love songs because I'm not in love. Instead, I write about my experiences, things that have embarrassed me, or things that irritate me. Writing is basically how I vent. 'There You Go' was a reflection of that – I'd always wanted to have the upper hand in that relationship, and the song was the only way I could achieve it."

Pink holds a writing credit on half the songs featured on her debut album (see the discography for detailed notes on all albums), a noteworthy achievement for a young artist entering the pop world. At a time when many pop stars relied heavily on outside songwriters, Pink's involvement in crafting her own music brought an added layer of authenticity to her work.

When pop stars contribute to their own songwriting, it often creates a deeper connection with audiences, as listeners can sense the personal experiences and genuine emotions woven into the lyrics.

For Pink, this authenticity would become a cornerstone of her brand, setting her apart from many of her contemporaries and establishing her as an artist with a strong, relatable voice. By sharing her perspective and emotions through her music, she invited fans to engage with her on a more personal level, laying the foundation for a career built on honesty and individuality.

'Most Girls' was released as the second single from Pink's debut album on 6th June 2000. This single was even more successful than the lead single, reaching the top ten in six countries. In Australia, it reached number one and was certified double Platinum by the Australian Recording Industry Association (ARIA). In Canada and New Zealand, it peaked at number two, earning Gold certification in both countries.

In the US, 'Most Girls' made its debut on the Billboard Hot 100 chart at number eighty-five on 12th August 2000. Three months later, it climbed to number four. It was Pink's highest-charting solo single in the US until 2008, when she would top the chart with 'So What.' Additionally, 'Most Girls' was her first single to top the Rhythmic radio chart. By November 2010, it would go on to sell 95,000 copies in the US.

The third single from Pink's debut album, 'You Make Me Sick' was released to American radio stations on 27th November 2000. It was the album's final single and didn't perform as well as the previous two, reaching number thirty-three on the Billboard Hot 100. However, it did better in other countries, peaking within the top ten in the UK, New Zealand, and the Netherlands. It was certified Gold in Australia.

By November 2010, 'You Make Me Sick' would go on to sell 93,000 copies in the US. The accompanying music video, filmed in late 2000, was directed by Dave Meyers. The single would also feature in the 2001 film and soundtrack, *Save The Last Dance*.

Released on 4th April 2000, *Can't Take Me Home* was met with mixed reviews. It achieved a reasonable extent of success on a global scale. In the US, it debuted and reached its peak at number twenty-six on the Billboard 200 chart (making it Pink's only studio album not to enter the top ten on this chart). The album remained on the chart for forty-nine weeks and ranked as the sixty-sixth best-performing album of 2000. It also made the Billboard year-end chart in 2001, reaching the ninety-eighth spot.

On the R&B/Hip Hop Albums chart, *Can't Take Me Home* reached number twenty-three, staying on the chart for fifty-five weeks and ranking as the eighty-seventh best-performing album on this chart in 2000. The album eventually achieved double Platinum certification from the RIAA, indicating two-million copies shipped in the US.

In Canada, the album peaked at number nineteen on the national album chart and reached number four on the Canadian R&B Albums chart. It was the thirty-third-best-selling album in Canada in 2000, and 177th in 2001. The album later received double Platinum certification from Music Canada for shipping 200,000 copies in the country.

Can't Take Me Home was more successful in Australia, where it reached number ten on the national album chart and topped the Australian R&B Albums chart. It was the thirty-second-best-selling album in Australia in 2000 and was later certified double platinum by ARIA for shipping 140,000 copies.

In New Zealand, the album peaked at number twelve on the national album chart and ranked as the forty-fourth-best-performing album of 2000. It eventually earned a Platinum certification from the Recording Industry Association of New Zealand for shipments of 15,000 copies.

In the UK, *Can't Take Me Home* peaked at number thirteen on the national album chart and was certified Platinum by the British Phonographic Industry. It was placed at number sixty-seven on the British year-end chart of 2000 and would go on to place at number 176 in 2011. The album also reached number three on the UK R&B Albums chart.

At the 2000 MTV Video Music Awards, Pink was nominated for Best New Artist. In the same year, at the Billboard Music Awards, she won the award for New Female Artist of the Year due to the success of *Can't Take Me Home* and its single. She also received nominations for Female Hot 100 Singles Artist and Female Artist of the Year at the Billboard Music Awards.

In 2001, Pink was nominated for Best International Female Solo Artist and Best International Newcomer at the Brit Awards. At the American Music Awards in the same year, she was nominated for Favourite Soul/R&B New Artist.

Interestingly, in *Rolling Stone*'s review of *Can't Take Me Home*, it was considered that there was no room for Pink's music amongst what was already available to the music-consuming public: "Pink is twenty-year-old Alecia Moore's hair dye of choice and, for that matter, her skin colour. She's got a dazzling, gymnastic R&B voice, without a hint of style that's all her own. Her debut has one awesome single in 'There You Go', whose wronged-woman sass is set to a stop-start groove so bling-bling it redeems a chorus that ends, 'Sometimes it beez like that.' Beyond that, though, every melismatic groan, every clipped harmony, every post-Timbaland beat, every synth setting (like the 'No Scrubs'-style harpsichord) is copped from some R&B hit of the last eighteen months. (The fiery internal dialogue of 'Split Personality' would have seemed more original before Kelis' 'Caught Out There', though.) She makes a pretty good Monica, but we already have one of those."

New Musical Express was similar in its approach to reviewing *Can't Take Me Home*; whilst there was praise overall for the album in and of itself, there was an element of caution in terms of questioning whether the world needed another solo female artist: "It's likely that nineteen-year-old Philadelphia resident Pink is going to become very famous indeed. With a million-dollar debut video, a team of R&B's most sought-after producers, her own "voice" and a street-tough urban "atttitood" that looks sooo cool on MTV, it's hard not to draw comparisons with that other white act currently doing very well off the back of black music..."

"Much like Marshall Mathers, Pink's debut is a slightly watered down take on the original flavour, but one that stands on its own thanks to her superb, effortless soprano. There's no doubting her star quality, it's just that this record doesn't capitalise enough on what's obviously a massive talent. Standout tracks include all tunes penned by Kevin 'She'kspere' Briggs – the shit-hot R&B producer that made Destiny's Child the world's greatest soul pop act."

"Sadly, Pink's debut is a little samey and suffers from the diva disease that modern R&B acts like Kelis are helping to stamp out. Like when an otherwise affecting ballad like 'Let Me Let You Know' is ruined by a calamitous descent into Mariah Carey warbling. Despite this, it's still an impressive debut – we await part two."

So, was there truly a glut of solo female artists around the time that Pink came onto the scene with her new album? Well, maybe. In 2000, the music industry was awash with pop icons and emerging female solo artists. The market was saturated with carefully crafted images, and the radio airwaves were dominated by an abundance of glossy, choreographed pop acts. However, whilst some critics might have dismissed Pink as just another name in a crowded field as part of arguing that the world didn't need yet another female solo artist, Pink would soon prove them wrong, establishing herself as a unique and indispensable presence in the popular music landscape.

While Pink's debut album contained elements typical of early-2000s pop and R&B, she immediately distinguished herself with her edgy style and rebellious attitude. Unlike other female solo artists who embraced a highly polished and glamorous image, Pink opted for a more raw and unconventional look. Her distinctive hair alone – a short, choppy, vibrant magenta, styled with a nod to punk – signalled that she wasn't interested in fitting into the industry's cookie-cutter mould. This unique branding caught the attention of listeners and set Pink apart from her contemporaries.

Beyond her style, Pink's attitude and persona would contribute to her rapid rise. Exuding a rebellious energy, challenging norms and defying expectations in an industry often criticised for its artificiality and emphasis on image, Pink's authenticity would prove her to be a breath of fresh air. Speaking openly about her life experiences, struggles, and views, she would continue to resonate with audiences who were seeking something more genuine. Critics who initially doubted her relevance would soon find themselves acknowledging her distinctive voice and undeniable charisma.

Glitter in the Air - *The Evolution of Pink*

CHAPTER TWO
HEY SISTER, GO SISTER

When production began on *Moulin Rouge!* (2001) in November 1999, esteemed filmmaker Baz Luhrmann set out to create a film that would not only entertain, but one that would immerse audiences in a world of vibrant colours, pulsating music, and intense emotion. The genesis of the film can be traced to Luhrmann's unique vision for what cinema can be, drawing on elements of theatre, opera, and pop culture to craft an experience that is at once familiar whilst being entirely new and original.

One of the most striking aspects of *Moulin Rouge!* is in its bold fusion of styles. Luhrmann combined elements of musical theatre, opera, and pop culture to create a film that defies easy categorisation. The soundtrack, featuring contemporary pop songs re-imagined in a theatrical context, played a central role in this fusion. Songs such as Elton John's 'Your Song' and 'Roxanne' by The Police were given new life through elaborate choreography and dramatic performances, bridging the gap between classic and modern.

At its core, *Moulin Rouge!* is a love story, but Luhrmann approached this theme with a sense of grandiosity and drama. The film explores the romance between Christian, a young writer, and Satine, a star performer at the Moulin Rouge. Luhrmann's intention was to create a love story that resonated on an emotional level while also embracing the larger-than-life elements of musical theatre. The narrative unfolds with a mixture of comedy, tragedy, and romance, keeping the audience on an emotional rollercoaster throughout.

The visual spectacle of *Moulin Rouge!* is another testament to Luhrmann's ambitious vision. The film's lavish sets, vibrant costumes, and elaborate choreography create a captivating sensory feast. Luhrmann's use of rapid editing, dynamic camera movements, and surreal imagery add to the film's energetic pace and theatrical flair. This innovative approach to cinematography and visual design would go on to largely account for the film's enduring appeal and its status as a modern classic.

Vitally, an elaborately grandiose film would call for a soundtrack capable of standing alongside it; a soundtrack that wouldn't pale in comparison. And that's where Pink comes into the picture.

At the start of the video for the 2001 cover of Labelle's 1974 hit 'Lady Marmalade', Missy Elliott (who co-produced the track with Rockwilder) stands in front of a red velvet curtain, inviting viewers to the Moulin Rouge and introducing the night's superstar line-up: Christina Aguilera, Pink, Lil' Kim, and Mýa. The four female pop icons, all at a high point in their respective careers, are iconic in their embracement of the almost-gaudy burlesque aesthetic: corsets, fishnet stockings, top hats, rhinestone-studded lingerie, glittering costume jewellery, lace-up boots, and colourful wigs aplenty.

A pioneer within hip-hop and R&B music, known for her innovative style and fearless approach, Missy Elliott felt that the collaboration was more than just a chance to work with other talented artists – it was an opportunity to honour a legendary song and infuse it with a fresh, modern twist. A fan of the original song, she saw the cover as a chance to pay tribute to a piece of musical history. She understood the significance of the track and was excited to be part of a project that would introduce it to a new generation of listeners. The cover presented a unique opportunity to celebrate the spirit of the original whilst adding a contemporary edge that would resonate with a new audience.

In 2001, both the 'Lady Marmalade' single and the supporting video served as a clear testimony to the collaborative spirit between the high profile artists. Christina Aguilera, Lil' Kim, Mya, Pink, and Missy Elliott all brought an exciting contribution to what would be a creative and energetic project ensuring that the cover of a classic song would be a dynamic and memorable re-imagining. By bringing together strong female voices from different musical backgrounds, the project emphasised the idea that strong women could collaborate and create something remarkable.

Each of the artists involved with 'Lady Marmalade' have gone on to express how excited they were to work on a piece with a strong theme of female empowerment. The original song was known for its unapologetic attitude and celebration of feminine strength, and the cover carried this message forward. Alongside the other female artists involved, Pink embraced this spirit of empowerment, infusing the song with confidence and energy. This celebration of female power and independence resonated with audiences, making the cover a hit on the charts and an iconic moment in pop culture.

In particular, Pink's presence in the group underscored this sense of unity, with her rebellious persona and edgy style adding a unique dimension to the mix. Her vocal style brought a raw energy to the track. Her distinctive voice, with its rock-infused edge, contrasted with the styles of her collaborators, creating a dynamic interplay that made the song exciting and unpredictable. This blend of voices mirrored the diversity of women in the music industry, reinforcing the message that female artists could embrace their individuality while coming together to create something powerful.

Pink's contribution added a layer of defiance and grit, aligning with the song's themes of independence and self-assurance. The music video, with its vibrant costumes and elaborate choreography, further emphasised this sense of empowerment, showcasing the artists in roles that exuded confidence and control. Pink's rebellious edge and fearless attitude were central to this visual representation, reminding viewers that women could be both strong and glamorous.

With her assertive vocal delivery and bold presence, Pink's contribution reinforced the idea that women could own their identity and embrace their power without apology. This reclamation of power resonated with audiences, as it challenged traditional gender roles and celebrated women's agency.

Interestingly, Pink's role in the 2001 cover of 'Lady Marmalade' would prove to be a precursor to the extents of female empowerment and autonomy that she would embrace for her second album.

In August 2001, Pink met professional motocross racer Carey Hart at the seventh X Games at the South Philadelphia Sports Complex. Hart had become a professional motorcyclist at eighteen and started competing in the AMA Supercross circuit. He was among the first riders to compete in freestyle motocross in 1996 and was the first to publicly perform the BMX trick known as the "Superman seat grab" at IFMA events in 1998-99. He was also the first person to perform the "invert Superman" seat grab at the 1999 Gravity Games in Providence, Rhode Island. As such, this trick is now referred to as the "Hart Attack." In 1999, Hart won the bronze medal at the Summer Gravity Games and gold at the Australian X Games. The following year, during the 2000 Gravity Games in Providence, Rhode Island, Hart attempted the first backflip on a 250cc motorcycle in competition.

At the same 2001 X Games where he met Pink, Hart attempted the backflip again, but it ended in a serious crash. He suffered multiple broken bones, fractured ribs, and a bruised tailbone. Hart was soon back to competing. At Moto X Big Air in 2002, he won silver, narrowly missing out on gold. Mike Metzger won with a score of 95, while Hart came close with 94.67.

Despite the intensity of the motocross world, it wasn't just Hart's daredevil stunts that left a lasting impression on Pink. Meeting him marked the start of a relationship that would soon become one of the most defining in her life.

CHAPTER THREE
THE SECOND IMPRESSION

It is not uncommon for musical artists to reach a point in their careers where they feel the need to explore new creative territories, diverging from the styles and themes that defined their earlier work.

Artists, like all creative individuals, evolve over time. The experiences they gather, both personally and professionally, shape their outlook and influence their work. As musicians mature, they often find that their earlier music no longer reflects their current perspectives or artistic interests. This internal evolution can lead to a natural inclination to explore new genres, themes, or collaborative ventures, providing a canvas for creative reinvention. Such changes can be gradual, with each album introducing subtle shifts, or more abrupt, with a radical departure from previous styles.

The music industry has a tendency to pigeonhole artists, encouraging them to stick to proven formulas and replicating past successes. While this approach may bring short-term commercial rewards, it can also stifle creativity and hinder artistic growth. When artists decide to break away from industry expectations, it's often a response to this pressure to conform. They may want to challenge themselves, expand their musical horizons, or push back against being typecast. This defiance of expectations allows artists to reclaim their creative agency and redefine their artistic identity.

The desire to break away from expectations often comes after a number of successful albums, when artists have established their place in the industry but seek to avoid stagnation and predictability. For Pink though, she had already reached this point following the release of her debut album.

By the time she began work on her second album, Pink had already achieved a significant level of success and recognition. *Can't Take Me Home* had garnered commercial success and established her as a unique voice in the pop music landscape. However, she was already facing a pivotal point in the relatively early stages of her career.

With hits like 'There You Go' and 'Most Girls' having climbed the charts and captured the attention of fans and industry insiders alike; Pink had already established herself as a rising star with a distinctive style and attitude. Notably, reaching this level of success early on can be a double-edged sword, creating pressure to replicate or exceed it with the second album. What makes Pink's journey so remarkable is her refusal to simply repeat the formula that brought her initial fame.

Although *Can't Take Me Home* was commercially successful, Pink felt unhappy and restricted due to her limited creative control and the way she had been marketed to a teen audience as an R&B singer. In an interview with MTV News in October 2000, Pink's father, Jim Moore, mentioned that she was interested in exploring different musical styles and demonstrating her versatility on her upcoming album, with desires to create a record that reflected the diverse musical influences she grew up with, similar to the sounds of artists like Annie Lennox and Method Man.

Frustrated with being marketed as just another cookie-cutter pop act, Pink was eager to be recognised as a more serious songwriter and musician, and to perform the type of music she truly wanted to create. To achieve this, she would change her sound and take greater artistic and creative control during the recording of her second album (which would ultimately end up being recorded in numerous locations: The Enterprise in Burbank, Pinetree Studios in Miami Beach, DARP Studios in Atlanta, Larrabee in North Hollywood, LP Studios in Sherman Oaks, Sony Studios in Santa Monica, and Drive By Studios in North Hollywood).

While on a 2001 photo shoot for *Teen*, Pink came across the phone book of her makeup artist, Billy Brasfield. In it, she found the number for Linda Perry, the lead singer of the former

American alternative rock band 4 Non Blondes.

Pink had grown up listening to their 1992 album, *Bigger, Better, Faster, More!*, and called Perry her "childhood idol." After noting down the number, Pink later left Perry a ten-minute message on her answering machine, expressing her admiration and explaining how much she loved Perry's music. She also joked that Perry "owes" her because she got arrested for singing her songs out of her window at 3:30 in the morning, and jokingly added that she would stalk Perry if she didn't return her call.

A few minutes after Pink had left the voicemail, Perry returned the call and invited Pink to her house in Los Angeles. When Pink proposed writing a song together, Perry was initially hesitant. In an interview with the *San Francisco Chronicle*, Perry mentioned that she told Pink, "I'm not hip at all. I make low-fi, garage-sounding classic rock records." Pink replied, "I know – that's what I want." After this exchange, Pink met Perry.

Recording sessions for Pink's second album started at Perry's home studio. Perry, playing piano, asked Pink to share her feelings through a melody. At first, Pink felt nervous and unsure, as she was used to a different creative process. As Perry played chords over a basic instrumental, Pink grabbed a microphone and began to improvise. Within about five minutes, they wrote and recorded 'Eventually.' The lyrics were spontaneous, and Pink's vocals were captured in a single take. Perry described the experience as emotional, noting that it helped Pink feel more at ease and understood during the recording process.

A week before meeting Pink, Perry had been working on a song called 'Get The Party Started.' Perry was not particularly familiar with modern music technology, so she called a friend for advice. Following this, she bought various pieces of equipment, including a Korg Triton synthesiser, an Akai MPC, a TASCAM DA-88 recorder, and Roland expansion cards.

She started experimenting with these tools, initially without a specific goal in mind. Perry programmed her first beat, utilising a bass guitar, a horn sample, and looping "weird chords and sounds." She finished the song by incorporating a variety of catchy phrases, later realising with a laugh that she had written her first dance song.

Confident of the song's commercial potential, Perry had attempted to offer 'Get The Party Started' to Madonna, but without success. Once the sessions with Pink began, Perry introduced the song to Pink, who agreed to record it.

Pink stayed at Linda Perry's home for several months, where they planned to write twenty-five songs for Pink's second album. They spent their time brainstorming and working on new ideas. The sessions at Perry's home studio produced about twenty tracks in six weeks, focusing on themes of introspection and emotional exploration. Working with Perry was a significant step in Pink's pursuit of greater artistic control over her music in how it facilitated her aim to move away from the R&B-orientated "marketing concept" of her first album.

About her working relationship with Pink, Perry said: "What happened was that we were able to open up to each other... she completely abandoned what she was told she was supposed to be and just became Alecia Moore."

"I went after people who inspired me, not the hot new record producer or anything," Pink said at the time. "It's all done very organically. I mean, I'm old-school to the bone, and this is a very artist-driven record, not a producer-driven record."

It was after signing with LaFace Records that Pink had first met producer Dallas Austin. Austin wasn't a fan of Pink's R&B direction, and their sessions for *Can't Take Me Home* had been largely unproductive. However, Pink was interested in working with him again for her second album. This time, they leaned into a pop rock sound, and the songs they created had an autobiographical tone.

Austin co-wrote and produced four songs for Pink's second album – '18 Wheeler', 'Don't Let Me Get Me', 'Just Like A Pill', and 'Numb'. Each of these songs features introspective lyrics. Austin encouraged Pink to be bolder in her songwriting, emphasising that crafting songs also involves shaping a specific attitude (which, of course, would all form a vital aspect of Pink's branding around that time).

Pink collaborated with Scott Storch, who had previously worked with the likes of Dr. Dre and Snoop Dogg, on 'Family Portrait', which began as a poem she wrote when she was nine years old. The track delves into her parents' divorce and her experiences growing up in a dysfunctional family. Reflecting on these themes, Pink noted how they impacted on her life and she decided to turn her feelings into a song. She explained that while it was painful, it also allowed her to release some of her emotions, adding, "Pain is not always a bad thing. It can be a learning thing."

Another collaborator on the album was Aerosmith's frontman, Steven Tyler. Pink, who considered Tyler one of her musical inspirations, met him at a radio show in New York. They quickly connected and decided to record a song together. 'Misery', written by Richie Supa and co-produced with Marti Frederiksen, was brought to Pink by Tyler, who said she "loved it." Pink described recording with Tyler as "an experience of a lifetime."

Pink had surprisingly begun working with Perry without the knowledge of her record label. After several sessions, she presented four songs to producer L.A. Reid, including 'Get The Party Started.' Although Reid saw potential in that song as a lead single, he rejected much of the other material. Two weeks later, Reid and Pink met in Miami, where Reid expressed concern about her shift away from the R&B sound that had characterised her debut album. He worried that this change could alienate her existing audience.

Pink's push for more creative control faced resistance, especially since she was a relatively new artist. Despite Reid's efforts to convince her to record more R&B tracks, Pink stood firm on her new direction. After a heated argument, Reid ultimately conceded and allowed Pink the "opportunity to fail." Despite his initial reservations, Reid later praised the completed album, calling it a "masterpiece" and expressing confidence that it would be a significant success.

Pink later discussed the risks of changing musical genres with the *Los Angeles Times*, acknowledging the potential challenges that could come with such a move: "I knew the risk involved. I'd seen artists change styles and fail miserably, but I've also seen artists change and continue to do well. That's why Madonna has always been an inspiration for me. I told [Reid] I had faith in my ability and I was willing to take the chance. And I have so much respect for him because he turned around during that meeting.

By the end, he said, 'okay, let's do it.'"

Pink's second album, *Missundaztood* is primarily in the vein of pop rock, but is infused with an eclectic mix of musical styles. It traverses genres like pop, rock, disco, R&B, blues, and hip hop, demonstrating Pink's broad musical palette. This fusion of styles creates a unique listening experience, where each track has its own character, yet the album maintains an enjoyably coherent quality.

Tracks like 'Don't Let Me Get Me' and 'Just Like A Pill' are driven by rock-influenced electric guitars, adding a raw energy to the album. The production melds a funky bass line with simple electric rhythm guitar and a spare synth line, creating a sound that is both familiar and innovative.

'Get The Party Started,' one of the album's most iconic tracks, features vocodered vocals and elements of dance pop and new wave. This high-energy song would quickly become a party anthem, with its infectious beat and catchy chorus. It's a masterclass in how to craft a pop anthem that is as infectious as it is enduring.

From the very first beat, the song grabs listeners with its pulsating, upbeat rhythm and irresistibly funky bass line. Pink's vocal delivery elevates the track further; her raspy tone and undeniable attitude infuse every lyric with charisma and swagger. The song was a perfect fit for the post-millennium pop landscape, where bold, genre-blurring tracks were redefining mainstream music.

'18 Wheeler' stands out for its arena rock influences and rock instrumentation, demonstrating Pink's ability to channel a heavier, more powerful sound.

The blues rock ballad 'Misery,' featuring a guitar solo by Bon Jovi's Richie Sambora, adds a gritty edge to the album. Pink's vocals are particularly expressive, conveying a raw emotion that complements the song's bluesy undertones. On 'Family Portrait,' Pink sings over a pop-R&B instrumentation combining a "snare" piano and strings, delving into personal themes and family dynamics.

Missundaztood takes listeners on a journey through diverse soundscapes. The album's penultimate track, 'Numb,' is an electropop song with grunge metal elements, evoking the sound of Nirvana with its distorted guitars and edgy vibe. The final track, 'My Vietnam', is a rock-neofolk ballad set to an acoustic guitar played by Linda Perry. This song's haunting melody and sonic interpolation of Jimi Hendrix's 'Star Spangled Banner' create a powerful conclusion to the album.

Missundaztood is a significant departure from Pink's debut, embracing a diverse range of musical styles and an edgier rock sound. The album's eclectic mix, from rock and blues to disco and hip hop, showcases Pink's versatility and artistic evolution, demonstrating her commitment to breaking away from expectations and creating music that is uniquely her own.

The lyrics on *Missundaztood* delve into personal themes like self-identity, loneliness, family issues, self-doubt, and rebellion. The album's title references Pink's feeling of being misunderstood. "I say the wrong things," she said. "I tell the truth, which tends to get me in trouble, and I'm a very eclectic person, so I feel that's misunderstood, as well."

The title track from *Missundaztood* is upbeat and energetic. In 'Don't Let Me Get Me', Pink opens up about her battles with feeling inadequate and experiencing self-loathing. The next song, 'Just Like A Pill', employs drug imagery to symbolise toxic relationships, also exploring themes related to substance abuse and personal insecurities.

Indeed, during her rebellious and turbulent formative years, Pink had been no stranger to drugs. On Thanksgiving in 1995, she overdosed in a Philadelphia nightclub. Allegedly, she had already been drinking beer, smoking marijuana, and using a cocktail of other substances, including ketamine, crystal meth, cocaine, ecstasy, and nitrous oxide. Apparently after taking large amounts of acid, her lips turned blue, and she lay on the floor, believing that it could be the end.

Prior to that fateful night, Pink had already lost several friends and acquaintances to drugs, but it was coming close to her own demise that served as the catalyst for change. She vowed to go clean, and she did it on her own, determined to stay in control.

Notably, 'Get The Party Started' contrasts with the album's more reflective themes, portraying a lively, self-assured woman in command. It's a celebration of fun, freedom, and self-assuredness, perfectly capturing the energy of a night out where anything feels possible.

'Respect' carries a message of female empowerment. '18 Wheeler' has lyrics that refer to enduring abuse before Pink declares that she won't be defeated. 'Family Portrait' explores family struggles, focusing on the tumultuous relationship between Pink's parents, which led to their divorce when she was no older than ten.

'Lonely Girl' conveys uncertainty and doubt through the song's lyrics. 'Dear Diary' delves into feelings of disillusionment and abandonment, while 'Numb' addresses the sorrow of a failed relationship. 'Gone To California' reflects on social issues.

The album's concluding track, 'My Vietnam', is about Pink's journey of self-discovery. Its lyrics examine the effects of her father's service in the Vietnam War and how it impacted upon both his life and Pink's. It could be considered that the imagery of battle serves as a metaphor for Pink's upbringing, of which she has often said there was turbulence in the form of her parents' arguing prior to their divorce.

Indeed, a veteran of the Vietnam War, Jim Moore was politically active (his wife, Pink's stepmother, had worked as a nurse caring for soldiers during the conflict).

After years of denying and staying silent about the horrors he had witnessed during the war, as he approached his fortieth birthday, Moore came to the decision that he needed to deal with the internal struggles he had faced since returning home. Establishing the Vietnam Veterans Chapter 210 of Bucks County, he was active in raising funds and offering group support sessions for veterans in the county.

As a young girl, Pink would accompany her father to these meetings, where she would witness grown men breaking down in tears. She also joined her dad in marches for veterans' rights and accompanied him while he served food at soup kitchens. Rather than feeling bored or uncomfortable, she found these activities inspiring.

"I respected my dad," she told *The Guardian* in 2006, "because he would put me through a wall if I didn't. He was consistent, and

I respected that. If he wanted to warn me, he'd count to three, but I only ever let him get to two-and-three-quarters. You don't fuck with Jim Moore – you just don't. He could kick your ass, he could make you laugh, or he could teach you something. He was a cool guy."

Missundaztood was released on 20th November 2001 through Arista Records. The album came out in several European countries on 28th January 2002, with a different track order and a bonus track titled 'Catch-22'. A deluxe edition was released on 26th November 2002, which included the original album on CD and a DVD featuring music videos for 'Family Portrait' and 'Don't Let Me Get Me'. This deluxe version also contained live performances of 'Numb' and 'Family Portrait' recorded at Scala in London. The album would go on to be released on vinyl in October 2017.

Four singles were released from *Missundaztood*: 'Get The Party Started' on 16th October 2001; 'Don't Let Me Get Me' on 18th February 2002; 'Just Like a Pill' on 10th June 2002; and 'Family Portrait' on 16th September 2002. All four singles reached the top twenty on the Billboard Hot 100, with the first three peaking in the top ten.

Pink promoted the album through various high-profile performances, including appearances at the Billboard Music Awards, the Kids' Choice Awards, the MTV Asia Awards, and the MTV Video Music Awards. She also made guest appearances on late-night television shows such as *The Late Show* with David Letterman, *Saturday Night Live*, and *The Tonight Show* with Jay Leno. For European promotion, Pink performed on *Wetten, dass..?* and at the MTV Europe Music Awards. To further support the album, Pink launched her first headlining tour, the Party Tour, in 2002.

Missundaztood debuted at number eight on the US Billboard 200 chart, selling 220,000 copies during the week of 8th December 2001. The album reached its highest position at number six on 26th January 2002 and remained on the chart for a total of ninety weeks.

In the US, *Missundaztood* was the sixth-best-selling album of 2002, with 3.1 million copies sold. It received a quintuple platinum certification from the Recording Industry Association of America (RIAA) on 22nd October 2003, for shipping five-million copies.

In Canada, *Missundaztood* peaked at number five on the Canadian Albums Chart and was also certified quintuple platinum by Music Canada (MC), indicating 500,000 copies shipped.

In the UK, *Missundaztood* debuted at number four on the UK Albums Chart, with first-week sales of 22,000 copies. It later peaked at number two during the week of 18th January 2003, almost a year after its release, held back from the top spot by Avril Lavigne's *Let Go*. By February 2023, the album had sold 1.88 million copies in the UK and earned a sextuple platinum certification from the British Phonographic Industry (BPI).

The album achieved its highest international chart position when it topped the Irish Albums Chart for the week ending 9th January 2003. It also peaked within the top five in various other countries, reaching number four in Austria, New Zealand, and Norway; and number five in Germany, Iceland, and the Netherlands.

Missundaztood received multi-platinum certifications in several regions, including double platinum in Germany and Switzerland, and quadruple platinum in Australia and New Zealand. By November 2003, the album had sold twelve-million copies worldwide.

Missundaztood garnered several award nominations, including Album of the Year at the 2002 Billboard Music Awards and Best Album at the 2002 MTV Europe Music Awards. It was also nominated for Favourite Pop/Rock Album at the 2003 American Music Awards and for Best International Album at the twenty-third Brit Awards.

At the forty-fifth Annual Grammy Awards in 2003, *Missundaztood* was nominated for Best Pop Vocal Album, and 'Get The Party Started' received a nomination for Best Female Pop Vocal Performance.

Missundaztood was met with generally positive reviews. *The Tampa Tribune* described the album as "an edgy, rock-driven set," praising its focus on "loneliness, family discord and [Pink's] refusal to fit in." *The Guardian* viewed it as "an unusually three-dimensional picture of growing up in a broken home," and found it "surprisingly good." *Billboard* called it "a rock-fused, hook-friendly set" and cited 'Numb' and 'Lonely Girl' as being indicative of Pink's versatility.

Rolling Stone cited the album as being "one of the most radical R&B-to-rock transformations since Prince abandoned disco for a *Dirty Mind* [(1980)]."

Endearingly, *Spin* noted how Pink's shift in musical direction on *Missundaztood* was reflective of her desire to assert her artistic independence and explore music on her terms. By embracing an eclectic mix of styles and infusing her music with personal themes, Pink crafted an album that was both innovative and deeply authentic.

The decision had proved itself to be a wise move in view of the fact that, according to some, *Missundaztood*'s release coincided with the declining popularity of heavily polished, bubblegum teen pop music. For instance, *The Guardian* attributed Pink's new popularity to the "lucrative and untapped market" of "teenage girls who may have liked Britney three years ago but now have a taste for low-key rebellion, the Osbournes and boys with tattoos."

The success of *Missundaztood* gave a significant boost to Linda Perry's career as a songwriter, leading her to collaborate with artists like Alicia Keys, Courtney Love, and Gwen Stefani. Perry recalled that her life "took a complete turn" after the release of *Missundaztood* and its lead single 'Get The Party Started,' and that working with Pink helped her discover that "helping artists with their vision is kind of cool."

So prolific was their songwriting partnership that Pink and Linda Perry contributed 'If You're Gonna Fly Away' to country singer Faith Hill's 2002 album, *Cry*.

Christina Aguilera would go on to mention that *Missundaztood* played a role in her decision to work with Linda Perry as a collaborator for her fourth studio album, *Stripped* (2002).

Looking back at what *Missundaztood* meant for her career, Pink would go on to tell *Variety* that it "was a huge turning point" in her life, adding, "before it came out, I was being told that it's going to completely fail. Still, I was stoked to be given the opportunity to fail."

Clearly, with *Missundaztood*, Pink chose to embrace a mindset that values artistic growth and experimentation over the fear of commercial rejection. Such perspective allowed her to push boundaries and explore new musical territories, accepting that failure could happen as a natural part of the artistic process.

At a stage in her career where many would have been afraid as to whether they would sink or swim following the debut album, Pink had the courage to take a risk – and in an industry that often prioritises predictability and formula as a route to success. Evidently, for Pink, in saying 'no' to what was expected of her, it paid off.

CHAPTER FOUR
A PARTY IN FULL SWING

While promoting *Missundaztood*, Pink expressed her pride in the album's fresh sound and her eagerness to hit the road. In planning the tour, she had full control over every aspect, including the staging and choice of opening acts.

At the ESPY Awards (Excellence in Sports Performance Yearly Award) Pink revealed that she had selected the all-female band Candy Ass because she had always wanted to be part of such a group. Additionally, she mentioned that she would be covering songs by her musical influences, including 4 Non Blondes, Aerosmith, Janis Joplin, Guns N' Roses and Mary J. Blige.

The stage design was relatively simple, featuring a backdrop that looked like a brick wall with the word 'P!nk' written in graffiti-style text. It also included a video screen, lights, instruments, and a single microphone. The setup was tailored for nightclubs and concert halls where Pink would be performing, which typically had an average audience size of three-thousand.

At the same time, Pink's contemporaries, Britney Spears and Christina Aguilera, were touring in larger venues like sports arenas and amphitheatres. Although Pink had previously dismissed comparisons to these artists, she addressed the difference in venue size by emphasising her own approach to touring.

"Big productions, to me, are great – I love going to Vegas and seeing shows," she told MTV, "but I think that sometimes it's distracting, especially when you are there to listen to the music… I love the shows that are in dingy little dark clubs, smoky, no production whatsoever. My stage show is raw and unpredictable. It's not a lot of choreography this time. There's practically no sequencing involved whatsoever. It's just instruments and a voice and incredible music. When there is a lot of sequencing or ProTools or DATs involved, it gets a little strange, so this is going to be definitely more organic."

Logistics and production style aside for a moment, by 2002, the pop music scene was in the midst of a dynamic transformation, and comparisons between Pink, Christina Aguilera, and Britney Spears had become a frequent topic of discussion. Each of these female artists had achieved significant commercial success, but their styles, personalities, and public personas set them apart in unique ways. Despite these differences, the comparisons emerged due to several key factors: their simultaneous rise to fame, their status as prominent female pop icons, and their differing approaches to the music industry.

All three artists became well-known during a period when the pop music scene was experiencing a resurgence driven by a new generation of young female artists. Pink had released *Can't Take Me Home* when Aguilera and Spears had already gained recognition with their earlier releases. Their concurrent successes then made them part of a broader cultural movement, inviting comparisons and discussions about their respective trajectories.

Aguilera and Spears were initially associated with a more traditional pop aesthetic, characterised by catchy hooks, elaborate dance routines, and glamorous imagery. Fortunately for Pink, she was known for her rebellious attitude, raw vocals, and rock-infused sound. She was unapologetic in her defiance of industry norms, positioning herself as the antithesis of the more polished and choreographed pop personas.

In 2002, comparisons between Pink, Christina and Britney were fuelled by the evolution and transition of the artists themselves. Christina Aguilera, for instance, was beginning to shed her "girl next door" image and embrace a more edgy and mature persona with the release of her *Stripped* album. Britney Spears was also evolving, moving from her early pop image towards a more complex and nuanced identity. Pink's own journey towards greater authenticity and artistic freedom contributed to these comparisons, as each artist navigated the pressures of the music industry in their own unique way.

During rehearsals for the Party Tour, Pink reached out to

Lenny Kravitz, joking that she was preparing to be the opening act on his upcoming North American tour. To back up her playful claim, she invited him to watch her rehearse and even sent him a pair of black and pink underwear with 'The P!nk/Lenny Tour' written on them.

After finishing her North American tour dates, Pink joined Kravitz's Lenny Live Tour as the opening act. Once her stint with Kravitz was over, she embarked on a mini-tour of Europe, performing in England, Ireland, and Germany. She then took her tour to Japan and New Zealand before joining the Rumba Festival to tour Australia.

The tour had a sponsor, Bally Total Fitness, resulting in the official name, 'Bally Total Fitness presents Pink's 'The Party Tour 2002." As part of the sponsorship, Bally Total Fitness introduced the 'Get Your Body Started' movement classes in over four-hundred of its locations across the US and Canada. These fitness centres also organised dance competitions featuring songs from *Missundaztood*.

The tour earned considerable acclaim from critics. Many highlighted Pink's dynamic energy during her performances in how she guided the audience through a lively mix of R&B, rock, and pop music. On account of Pink's stage presence and versatility, some critics compared her to Madonna.

"Chrissie Hynde she's not, but somewhere between Shirley Manson and Madonna, Pink's rock-star niche is a natural," the *Boston Phoenix* opined. "Pink's material may not be revolutionary art, but revolution, however vaguely imagined, was clearly a theme. She gave the girls some grown-up stuff to think about, and it wasn't heavy on how to be a twenty-first-century "bimbo.""

Indeed, the review made a well-observed consideration of Pink's star persona. By not basing her image on appearing dumb and hyper-sexualised, Pink was at the pinnacle of a wave of female artists who redefined what success could look like in pop music. In her demonstration of how an artist could achieve commercial success and critical acclaim without compromising their authenticity or conforming to industry pressures, Pink's success challenged the music industry's more traditional standards, showing that a strong, empowered image could resonate with audiences and lead to a lasting impact.

Glitter in the Air - *The Evolution of Pink*

CHAPTER FIVE
FEEL GOOD, REAL GOOD

Pink would once again take centre stage with another lead single for a film soundtrack; this time, the 2003 film, *Charlie's Angels: Full Throttle*. 'Feel Good Time' is a high-energy track that encapsulates the action-packed, adrenaline-fuelled essence of the Charlie's Angels film franchise. Pink's involvement in this project demonstrated her adaptability and skill at creating music that would resonate with both movie audiences and pop music fans.

Charlie's Angels: Full Throttle was a sequel to the successful *Charlie's Angels* (2000) film (itself being derived from the successful TV series that ran 1976-1981), known for its mix of action, comedy, and strong female leads (with an ensemble cast of Cameron Diaz, Drew Barrymore and Lucy Liu in the lead roles). Pink's 'Feel Good Time' was an ideal fit for this, delivering a bold and energetic vibe that matched the film's high-octane sequences. The song's infectious beat and catchy melody added to the film's playful yet empowering atmosphere, making it a perfect soundtrack for the dynamic adventures of the Angels.

'Feel Good Time' was written by William Orbit and Beck Hansen, adding to the song's unique appeal. The song had initially been written and recorded by Beck and William Orbit as a track for Beck. However, when Pink expressed interest in covering it, Beck agreed to let her record the song. Beck's vocals and a guitar were removed from the original recording and replaced with Pink's vocals. Beck's version would later be made available on Orbit's website.

Orbit's production expertise and Beck's innovative songwriting complemented Pink's distinctive vocal style, creating a track that stood out from typical movie soundtracks. This collaborative effort contributed to the song's success, and served to reinforce Pink's reputation as an artist who could bring her own flavour to any project when collaborating with a diverse range of talents.

Pink's unique style and edge played a significant role in shaping 'Feel Good Time.' She brought a sense of attitude and energy to the song. The track's driving rhythm and Pink's confident vocal delivery captured the spirit of the film, highlighting the themes of female empowerment and camaraderie among the Angels. The song's lyrics, with their playful and carefree tone, resonated with audiences who appreciated the combination of action and fun that defines the *Charlie's Angels* franchise.

Released in May 2003 as the lead single for the *Charlie's Angels: Full Throttle* soundtrack, 'Feel Good Time' garnered widespread attention, becoming a chart-topping hit in several countries (the single peaked at number sixty on the US Billboard Hot 100, and at number three on the UK Singles Chart. It went on to be certified gold by the Australian Recording Industry Association, where it got to number seven). Receiving significant airplay on radio stations and music channels, its infectious rhythm made it a summer anthem. In 2004, it would go on to be nominated for a Grammy Award for Best Pop Collaboration with Vocals.

The song's popularity extended beyond the film's audience, attracting fans of Pink and those who enjoyed its upbeat, feel-good mood, which is particularly evident in the hook melodies. Lyrically, the song continued Pink's tradition of promoting empowerment and independence in her music; whilst its playful tone matched the light-hearted action of the film, its underlying message of embracing life and enjoying the moment resonated with Pink's broader themes of self-expression and confidence.

The commercial success and musical merit of the single would provide Pink with a solid platform to build upon as she prepared for the release of her third album, *Try This*.

When Pink began working on her third studio album following the success of *Missundaztood* and her global Party Tour, her aim was to build on the rock sound she had embraced on *Missundaztood*. To achieve this, she sought out producers and writers experienced in that genre.

Most of the tracks on *Try This* were produced and co-written by Tim Armstrong, the singer and guitarist from the punk band Rancid, who Pink had met through a mutual friend at a Transplants music video shoot. They immediately connected, leading Pink to co-write ten songs with Armstrong in a week while the Transplants were on tour with the Foo Fighters.

Eight of these tracks made it onto *Try This*, along with three songs written with Linda Perry, who had contributed significantly to *Missundaztood*. *Try This* also features a collaboration with electroclash artist Peaches, titled 'Oh My God.' 'Feel Good Time' was included as a non-US bonus track.

Try This would be Pink's final studio album under Arista Records. In 2006, she would go on to mention feeling dissatisfied with the pressure from the label to create an album after the success of *Missundaztood*. "I was kind of rebelling against the label on that one," she said. "I was going: 'You want a record? Fine, I'll write ten songs in a week for your fuckin' record and you can press it up and put it out."

She would also go on to describe the promotional efforts for the album as a difficult experience, saying, "I was walking out of half my interviews crying. I just felt they were putting a quarter in the slot to watch the monkey dance."

One of the primary complexities that arise when a musician becomes successful is the pressure to maintain that success. Record labels, driven by financial interests, often view successful artists as valuable assets and seek to capitalise on their popularity. This can result in demands for more frequent releases, extensive touring, and intense promotional schedules. The pressure to maintain a high level of output can be overwhelming for artists who value the creative process and need time to develop their work.

The artistic process is inherently fluid and requires space for experimentation, reflection, and inspiration, all of which were vital to the creation of *Missundaztood*. However, record labels may have rigid schedules and deadlines, expecting artists to consistently deliver chart-topping hits. This can create a challenging dynamic for musicians who want to explore new directions or take risks with their music. The pressure to conform to commercial expectations can stifle creativity and limit artistic growth, leaving artists feeling trapped in a cycle of producing formulaic songs that cater to the label's demands.

The pressure from record labels to continuously produce new music can take a toll on an artist's mental health and well-being. The demands can lead to burnout, stress, and exhaustion. This impact on an artist's mental health can further complicate the relationship with the record label, as the artist may struggle to meet expectations while dealing with the emotional and physical strain of the industry's demands. In such regard, it is entirely understandable as to how the promotional period for *Try This* was an unhappy and frustrating time for Pink.

In her decision to leave Arista, Pink's actions are indicative of her choosing to give herself more autonomy in the artistic process – a crucial step for many musicians who wish to maintain a sustainable career in the industry.

Try This came with a Parental Advisory warning, where the album was released as both an explicit version and an edited version.

Ironically, perhaps, in the early 2000s, albums bearing the Parental Advisory warning became symbols of intrigue and rebellion for teenagers. These explicit content labels, intended to alert parents and guardians to potentially inappropriate language and themes, had the unintended effect of attracting the attention of young listeners.

For teenagers, buying an album with a Parental Advisory warning was a way to assert their independence, embrace their rebellious streak, and connect with music that felt edgy and controversial. To own an album or single displaying the Parental Advisory warning, with its stark black-and-white design, became something of a badge of honour for many teenagers.

The early 2000s saw the rise of artists whose work frequently carried the Parental Advisory warning. Eminem, one of the most controversial and successful artists of the time, exemplified how controversy could drive record sales.

His albums, such as *The Marshall Mathers LP* (2000) and *The Eminem Show* (2002), were rife with explicit language and provocative themes, sparking public debates and criticism. Yet, this controversy only fuelled his popularity, with teenagers flocking to buy his albums, drawn by the rebellious energy and raw honesty he embodied. Eminem's success proved that controversy could be a powerful marketing tool, attracting attention and generating record sales.

Eminem was not the only artist to gain popularity through controversy. Other acts across a range of genres, such as Limp Bizkit, Linkin Park, and Korn, to name just a few, also released albums with the Parental Advisory label, contributing to the growing appeal of explicit content in music. The Parental Advisory warning became a symbol of authenticity, indicating that the artist was unafraid to explore darker themes and confront taboo topics.

The influence of the Parental Advisory warning extended beyond music, seeping into fashion and popular culture. T-shirts and merchandise featuring the iconic label became popular among teenagers, serving as fashion statements. These garments were worn as a way to express individuality and a sense of nonconformity, further emphasising the appeal of the warning label. By sporting the Parental Advisory sign, teenagers could signal their alignment with the edgier side of music and culture, reinforcing their identity as someone who desired to court controversy.

So, did Pink intentionally make an album that would need to display the Parental Advisory label? Well, not necessarily. Even prior to *Try This*, her approach to songwriting was such that the lyrics explored the complexities of her own life, including the challenges of growing up, the pain of broken relationships, and the search for self-acceptance. Inevitably, perhaps, the themes that she would continue to explore would naturally come with raw language and honest emotion.

Try This represents a bold and eclectic fusion of musical genres. At its core, the album is a pop/rock creation, yet it branches out to include diverse influences such as punk rock, R&B, new wave, and disco. This genre-blending approach showcases Pink's versatility as an artist and her willingness to explore new directions, creating a collection of songs that are vibrant, energetic, and engaging.

As the album's opening track, 'Trouble' is bursting with high-octane energy, featuring raw guitar riffs, driving drums, and Pink's powerhouse vocals. The song's punk rock edge contributes to its rebellious attitude, setting the tone for the album's bold approach. This pop/rock essence is woven throughout the album, providing a dynamic framework upon which Pink builds her exploration of various musical styles.

'Trouble' is attention-grabbing with its fast-paced tempo and aggressive instrumentation. This punk energy adds a rebellious spirit to the album, echoing Pink's own persona and her refusal to conform to traditional pop norms. The rawness and urgency of these punk elements lend *Try This* a distinctive edge, while infusing it with Pink's signature attitude.

'God Is A DJ' is an energetic and uplifting track that encapsulates Pink's rebellious spirit and dance-friendly style. The song combines driving beats, infectious melodies, and a powerful sense of freedom, inviting listeners to embrace the joy of music and to live life with intensity. Through the song, Pink explores themes of self-expression, liberation, and the transformative power of music, reminding us all to dance like nobody's watching.

At its core, 'God Is A DJ' is a celebration of music and life. The title metaphorically suggests that music can serve as a spiritual force, uniting people on the dance floor and allowing them to connect on a deeper level. With the lyric, "If God Is a DJ, life is a dance floor," Pink draws a parallel between the ecstasy of a great night out and the joy of living life to the fullest.

The lyric also emphasises the idea that life itself is a space for self-expression and creativity, where each individual has the power to create their own narrative. This message of liberation aligns with Pink's larger body of work, known for its themes of empowerment and rebellion. The song's celebratory feel is amplified by its uplifting tempo and vibrant production, providing a high-energy anthem that would go on to become a fan favourite.

While *Try This* is rooted in pop/rock, it also incorporates elements of R&B, adding a soulful depth to the album. 'Catch Me While I'm Sleeping' and 'Love Song' showcase a smoother, more melodic side of Pink's vocal style, with lush harmonies and a laid-back groove. These R&B influences provide a contrast to the album's more intense rock moments, demonstrating Pink's ability to navigate different genres with ease and grace.

The new wave and disco elements on *Try This* bring a touch of nostalgia and playfulness to the album. 'Humble Neighborhoods' features upbeat rhythms, funky bass lines, and synthesisers that evoke the sounds of the late 1970s and early 1980s. This incorporation of new wave and disco creates a lively and danceable atmosphere, adding a layer of fun and exuberance to the album's overall feel.

Despite Pink's displeasure with the record label whilst working on *Try This*, evidently, she succeeded to craft an album that is both edgy and soulful, capturing the essence of pop rock whilst embracing a wider range of influences.

Released as the first single from *Try This*, 'Trouble' was originally written by Tim Armstrong for his band Rancid in 2003. It achieved notable success in Canada, where it reached number two, and in the UK and Australia, where it landed in the top ten. In the US, it reached number sixty-eight on the Billboard Hot 100. The song's music video is western-themed. It was directed by Sophie Muller.

In 2003, 'Catch Me While I'm Sleeping' was released as a promotional single in the US, and during the same period, a promotional CD-R acetate of 'Humble Neighborhoods' was distributed in the UK. The follow-up single, 'God Is A DJ,' failed to chart on the Billboard Hot 100, but it did reach number eleven in the UK.

In 2004, 'Last To Know' was released exclusively in Europe, where it peaked at number twenty-one on the UK Singles Chart. The promotional music video is a compilation of scenes from Pink's concerts during her Try This tour in Europe. Directed by Russell Thomas, the video includes footage from shows in the Netherlands and London, capturing Pink's performance of the song, as well as other moments from these live appearances.

Released in November 2003, *Try This* hit the top ten in thirteen countries, including the US, where it peaked at number nine on the Billboard 200 chart (with first-week sales of 147,000 copies). In the UK, it reached number three, and in Canada, it got to number eight. It was certified Platinum in the US by the RIAA for shipments of over one-million copies. In Australia, it got to number eight and would once again enter the album chart there in June 2009.

Reviews were generally positive, with *Entertainment Weekly* calling it "a hooky, engaging throwaway that expands Pink's range while holding on fiercely to her irascible inner child."

By the time Pink embarked on her Try This tour, she had established herself as a formidable presence in the pop music world. With three albums under her belt – *Can't Take Me Home*, *Missundaztood*, and *Try This* – she had amassed a diverse repertoire that allowed for a highly versatile live performance. This versatility was a key aspect of her tour, enabling her to showcase a range of musical styles, emotional tones, and stagecraft elements. Pink's ability to draw from a rich catalogue of songs made the Try This tour an engaging and dynamic experience for her audience.

The show was divided into four acts, each representing Pink's three albums and an acoustic segment. During the first act, focusing on her debut album, Pink wore a large pink Mohican hairstyle, reminiscent of her pink-haired R&B days. In the second act, highlighting *Missundaztood*, she donned a long blonde wig and a red leather jacket.

For the acoustic segment, Pink changed into a long blue, red, and white dress. In the fourth act, supporting *Try This*, she removed the wigs and took on a rock-chick style outfit. In the encore, she wore an ensemble appropriate for a cover of Guns N' Roses' 'Welcome To The Jungle'. For the finale, she performed 'Get The Party Started' while elevated in the air.

CHAPTER SIX
EMOTIONALLY INVESTED

Having parted ways with Arista Records, Pink began experimenting with new sounds and collaborating with new producers for her fourth studio album, which was recorded between December 2004 and July 2005. Serving as executive producer, she worked with several other producers, including Billy Mann, Butch Walker, Dr. Luke and Max Martin.

Also during this time, doing away with convention, Pink proposed to Carey Hart. The pair had briefly separated in 2003, but by June 2005 she was adamant he was the man for her. During a motocross race in Mammoth Lakes, Pink wrote "Will U Marry Me?" on a pit board. He either didn't notice or ignored it and continued for another lap. She then added "Serious!" to the board, at which point he pulled off the track to accept – although she insisted he finish the race. They married in Costa Rica on 7th January the following year.

Back to the music and Pink would go on to explain the title of her fourth album, *I'm Not Dead*, in multiple interviews. Speaking to CBS News, she said it reflects a sense of being alive, spirited, and unwilling to "sit down and shut up," even when others might prefer that. In other interviews, she mentioned that the title was inspired by an "awakening," influenced by her turning twenty-five, and by her father having suffered a heart attack. The events caused a shift in Pink's perspective; she told *The Independent* that they had led her to care less about personal drama and more about the world in a broader sense.

Pink also described the album's title as stemming from an epiphany – one where she realised that she had a lot to learn about adult responsibilities and everyday realities. While she had found the recording process for *Try This* exhausting, she said she felt compelled to be "almost emotionally involved" when working on *I'm Not Dead*. She stated, "I guess I was just kind of at that place where I felt like I had something to add to the world. I feel like there's a hole, and I know how to fill it – people aren't talking trash anymore."

The emotional burst of inspiration helped Pink to make a stronger creative investment in making her fourth album, the result being one that she would be proud of. Such was her enthusiasm at the time, that she went on to estimate that she must have written over forty songs in preparation for the album, exploring every topic she could think of.

I'm Not Dead is primarily a pop album, but it incorporates a mix of acoustic, folk rock, hard rock, power pop, pop rock, folk pop, new wave, dance, and hip-hop elements.

The opening track, 'Stupid Girls', was inspired by Pink's observation of a lack of positive role models for young girls and her concern that many aspire to be like female pop icons, especially those near her Los Angeles home. Pink remarked that "the world is being fed a certain thing," and that her song aims to encourage young girls to develop independence and offer them choices.

'Who Knew' explores themes surrounding "the death of friendship," and it also addresses friends of Pink who died from drug overdoses. The song refers to multiple people. The third track, 'Long Way To Happy', is based on a poem about sexual abuse that Pink wrote when she was thirteen years old. She mentioned that many people she knew had been abused or mistreated by someone close to them, and that she was no exception.

The ballad 'Nobody Knows' conveys thoughts and ideas that people might have but don't outwardly show, with Pink describing it as the most vulnerable track on the album. Written by Pink and co-written and produced by Billy Mann, the song is a piano ballad dealing with feelings of depression.

Written and produced by Pink and Billy Mann, and featuring folk rock duo Indigo Girls, 'Dear Mr. President' is an open letter to then-President of the United States, George W. Bush. The song features a series of rhetorical questions aimed at the president, focusing on his views on issues like war, homosexuality, homelessness, and drug abuse.

A powerful and impactful song, 'Dear Mr. President' takes a direct and unflinching approach to addressing social and political issues. With poignant lyrics and a raw acoustic arrangement, the song stands out as a compelling piece of musical activism that resonates with listeners seeking a voice for social justice and accountability.

The song's power lies in its direct confrontation with political leadership. Pink does not shy away from asking hard-hitting questions, challenging the president. The lyrics are candid and unapologetic, illustrating Pink's willingness to use her platform to speak truth to power. This straightforward approach, combined with the personal tone of the lyrics, creates a sense of urgency and emotional intensity that is both engaging and thought-provoking.

'Dear Mr. President' is more than just a critique – it's a call for accountability. The lyrics demand answers from those in positions of power, emphasising the need for empathy and justice. For instance, "How do you sleep while the rest of us cry?" and "How do you dream when a mother has no chance to say goodbye?" brings attention to the human impact of political decisions.

The sixth track and title song, 'I'm Not Dead', is, according to Pink, her first "subtle" and "poetic" self-written piece. She described it as being more understated and nuanced than her usual style, which she acknowledged had a tendency to be more direct and blunt. The inspiration for the song came from the emotions that Pink and producer Billy Mann felt as their working relationship came to an end, capturing the uncertainty and fear of change.

'Cuz I Can' is about Pink playing by her own rules and boasts about her "bling," which contrasts with the anti-consumerist theme in 'Stupid Girls'. Pink was accepting of the noticeable inconsistency by going on to call herself "a walking contradiction" and "a hypocrite sometimes." Similarly, 'Leave Me Alone (I'm Lonely)' addresses conflicting emotions within a relationship. Pink would explain that she often experiences these contradictions, saying, "That's how I live my life. I'm a walking conflict." The song humorously reflects a need for personal space despite a deep love for her partner.

'U + Ur Hand' is a kiss-off song aimed at a man trying to be seductive. It became popular among fans before the album's release when it was leaked online. Pink wrote the song with Max Martin, Luke Gottwald, and Rami. It mocks the men who would flirt with Pink in clubs, with the title referring to the line "looks like it's just me and my hand tonight," which was a phrase she had heard being used by such men upon them being rejected.

Unsurprisingly, the song would cause controversy in the US due to its references to masturbation, with some radio stations declining to play it. Pink and her publicist would also go on to state that she had been forbidden from singing 'U + Ur Hand' on *American Idol*. Upon being asked to change the title and lyrics to 'U + Ur Heart', Pink had told them, "You want me to rewrite my song for you? For American fucking Idol? What does that even mean, how do you have sex with your heart?" Consequently, she would perform 'Who Knew' instead.

Pink would go on to say that 'Runaway' was hard for her parents to hear because it delved into her experiences and feelings that her parents hadn't been aware of. Despite the intense subject matter, Pink would reassure her mother that some of the content was exaggerated for dramatic effect.

'The One That Got Away' explores the classic question of whether the grass is greener on the other side, while 'Conversations With My 13 Year Old Self' is a deeply personal track where Pink reflects on her younger, "pissed-off, complicated" self. She spoke of how writing this song was therapeutic for her, in how she imagined how her younger self might react to a hug – initial resistance followed by a collapse into tears.

'Fingers' is about self-pleasure. Although Pink would acknowledge that *I'm Not Dead* might have featured too many songs on the topic, she said that she couldn't resist.

The album's final track, a hidden bonus called 'I Have Seen The Rain', was written by Pink's father, James Moore, when he was a soldier during the Vietnam War. Pink had always wanted to record it with him and, for the album, learned to harmonise with him in order to make it possible. She would describe the recording experience as "adorable," noting that her father was incredibly nervous, all of which made it a special moment for them to share.

Before 'Stupid Girls' was selected as the lead single from *I'm Not Dead*, music videos were filmed for both 'Stupid Girls' and 'U + Ur Hand', the latter becoming the album's third single.

Pink mentioned that for the 'U + Ur Hand' video, she went for a "glammed" look, with each different appearance taking four hours of makeup and one hour of shooting. She wanted the video to be visually vibrant and colourful. In the bedroom scene, her outfit was made from pieces of black lace imported from France, costing three-hundred US dollars per yard of fabric.

Released in spring 2006, 'Stupid Girls' reached number thirteen on the US Billboard Hot 100 and entered the top five in the UK and Australia. The song generated significant attention, with Pink discussing the so-called "stupid girl epidemic" on *The Oprah Winfrey Show*. 'Stupid Girls' was nominated for a Grammy Award for Best Female Pop Vocal Performance, and its music video, directed by Dave Meyers, won an MTV Video Music Award for Best Pop Video.

'Who Knew' was released as the second single from *I'm Not Dead* in May 2006. Initially, it failed to chart on the US Billboard Hot 100. However, the song later appeared on the chart in March 2007 after it was used to promote the ABC television show *October Road*. It was re-released in the US in June 2007, ultimately reaching number nine on the Hot 100 by mid-September. 'Who Knew' also made it into the top ten in other countries, including Australia and the UK.

The third single, 'U + Ur Hand', took three months to chart on the Hot 100 but later peaked at number nine in April 2007. It also reached the top twenty in most European countries and Australia between August and September 2006.

The fourth single, 'Nobody Knows', was released outside the US in November 2006 and reached the top forty in both the UK and Australia.

'Dear Mr. President' received significant attention, leading fans to believe it might be released as a single. However, Pink decided against releasing it as an official single, stating that she didn't want people to think it was just a publicity stunt. Despite this, an acoustic version of the song was released as a downloadable single in Belgium in late 2006, reaching number one on the Ultratop chart.

In the UK, 'Dear Mr. President' was issued as a download-only single alongside 'Leave Me Alone (I'm Lonely),' making it into the UK top forty. The song also reached the top five in Australia, becoming the fifth track from *I'm Not Dead* to achieve that measure of success.

Released in April 2006, the album itself sold 126,000 copies in its first week in the US and debuted at number six on the Billboard 200, marking a higher initial position than Pink's previous two albums, *Missundaztood* and *Try This*, though with lower first-week sales. *I'm Not Dead* remained on the chart for a total of eighty-eight non-consecutive weeks, with its final week being in December 2009.

In the UK, *I'm Not Dead* debuted at number three, selling 39,892 copies. It became the ninth-best-selling album of 2006, with over 848,000 copies sold that year. It would re-enter the UK top 100 album chart at number ninety-nine in October 2007.

In Australia, *I'm Not Dead* reached number one after twenty-six weeks of release, becoming Pink's first album to top the Australian ARIA chart. It returned to the number one spot in its sixty-first week and set a record by spending sixty-two consecutive weeks in the top ten. It was Australia's second-best-selling album in both 2006 and 2007, and it was the country's top-selling album by an American or female artist in each of those years.

In Canada, the album debuted at number two with 13,000 copies sold in its first week, and the Canadian Recording Industry Association (CRIA) certified it Platinum for shipments exceeding 100,000 copies. In Germany, *I'm Not Dead* became Pink's first album to reach the number one spot.

I'm Not Dead was met with generally positive reviews. *Rolling Stone* considered that it "swaggers with a cockiness that most dudes in bands can't match. Whether she sings rock, pop, R&B, or her usual combination of all three, the twenty-six-year-old Doylestown, Pennsylvania, native is belting more urgently and taking more risks than her pop-radio contemporaries."

Indeed, due to its fearless exploration of a wide range of

controversial and challenging themes, lyrically, *I'm Not Dead* was Pink's boldest album at that point in her career. The honesty she embraced, along with the willingness to tackle personal struggles, societal issues, political commentary, and complex relationships, made it a significant milestone. With this album, Pink proved that no subject was off the table, solidifying her reputation as an artist who exuded authenticity and was unafraid to use her platform to speak out on important issues.

Pink's I'm Not Dead Tour in North America began on 24th June 2006, in Chicago and concluded in Dallas after a total of twenty shows. Her European tour started on 8th September of the same year in Istanbul, comprising fifty-two shows and scheduled to end in Milan on 21st December. A DVD recording from one of these European concerts, *Pink: Live From Wembley Arena*, was released in April 2007.

In 2007, Pink returned to the US to join Justin Timberlake on the first leg of his FutureSex / LoveShow tour. That same year, she launched her Australian tour in April, which quickly sold out. The Australian leg set a record with thirty-five arena shows, selling approximately 307,000 tickets, making it the most successful arena tour by a female artist in Australian history.

Sony BMG Australia released a special tour edition of *I'm Not Dead* in March 2007. It contained the original album along with two bonus tracks and a DVD with live performances and music videos. In December of the same year, a special edition was released in the US under the title of *Platinum Edition*, featuring additional DVD content not included in the Australian version.

During the period of 2006 to 2007, Pink collaborated with numerous other artists and expanded her musical reach. She appeared on the Indigo Girls album *Despite Our Differences*, contributing to their folk-rock sound. She also collaborated with India Arie on 'I Am Not My Hair', which was used in the Lifetime Television film, *Why I Wore Lipstick To My Mastectomy*.

Pink also recorded a track with Annie Lennox and twenty-two other female artists for Lennox's fourth solo studio album, *Songs Of Mass Destruction*. This song, titled 'Sing', was described by Lennox's website as an anthem for HIV/AIDS awareness and advocacy.

Pink's songwriting skills were also in demand. She wrote 'I Will' for Belgian singer Natalia's third album, *Everything And More*. Another of her co-written songs, 'Outside Of You', was recorded by dance-pop singer Hilary Duff and included on Duff's 2007 album, *Dignity*.

Overall, the *I'm Not Dead* period of Pink's career achieved levels of success that solidified her rising stardom. The album's commercial performance, critical acclaim, and cultural impact demonstrated that Pink was not only maintaining her place in the industry but also reaching new heights.

Taking into account that Pink poured so much emotional investment into making the album, *I'm Not Dead* highlighted her ability to strike a balance between commercial appeal and artistic integrity.

Pink's fearless approach, with her bold lyrical themes, and her ability to connect with a broad audience – both on record and on-stage – proved to be key factors in her ascent, positioning her as a star whose influence and popularity would continue to grow.

CHAPTER SEVEN
STILL A ROCK STAR

By 2008, the landscape of pop music had shifted noticeably from the time when Pink had first emerged on the scene in the early 2000s. This period of change reflected evolving musical trends, emerging technologies, and a broader cultural context that influenced the way pop music was created, distributed, and consumed.

One of the most significant changes was the rise of digital music. The increasing popularity of platforms such as iTunes and other digital download services transformed the way music was purchased and consumed.

This shift had a profound impact on the industry, leading to the decline of physical album sales and a focus on individual tracks and singles. Artists had to adapt to this new environment, where, to an extent, the success of a song could be measured by its download and streaming numbers rather than traditional album sales.

Social media platforms like MySpace, Facebook, and YouTube were becoming key drivers in how people could consume music. The platforms allowed artists to connect directly with their fans, share music and videos, and promote their work. This change provided new opportunities for artists to build their fan base and gain visibility, but it also meant that the music industry was becoming more democratised and competitive. For established artists like Pink, the rise of social media required a strategic approach to maintain relevance and engage with a rapidly changing audience.

The musical styles that dominated pop music in 2008 were also different from those of the early 2000s. While pop music still maintained its core elements of catchy melodies and infectious rhythms, there was a greater influence from electronic and dance music.

Artists like Lady Gaga and Katy Perry were emerging with a sound that blended pop with dance beats, signalling a shift towards a more electronic-oriented style. This change influenced the production of pop music, leading to a more synthesised and polished sound compared to the rawer, rock-infused elements that had characterised Pink's earlier work.

Fortunately for Pink, by this time, she had established herself as pop rock royalty. Thanks to her previous albums and tours, she had an enthusiastically loyal fan base. Having earned her strong following through her unique approach to music, her fearless attitude, and her ability to connect with audiences through her unapologetic and authentic storytelling, she already had a level of success and loyalty from fans that would provide a significant advantage as she navigated what to create for what would be her fifth album.

A lot had happened in Pink's personal life since the release of *I'm Not Dead* in 2006. Much of this would inform her approach to making album number five, which, after much consideration, would go on to be titled *Funhouse*.

After several months of speculation, Pink confirmed in February 2008 that she and her husband had separated. Her publicist stated, "Pink and Carey Hart have separated. This decision was made by best friends with a huge amount of love and respect for one another. While the marriage is over, their friendship has never been stronger." During their separation, the couple attended marriage counselling in an attempt to reconcile.

Pink wrote and recorded about thirty to thirty-five songs for *Funhouse*. Choosing which tracks would make it onto the album was challenging, as she described it as "like getting rid of your children." She explained that she had to think of the selection process in terms of "I like that one too, but I'm going to let that one die." The advantage, Pink noted, was in how different countries would request additional songs and B-sides, providing a place for the other "children."

To write and record *Funhouse*, Pink travelled internationally, collaborating with Eg White in London, and Max Martin in Stockholm. Reflecting on these sessions, Pink said it was beneficial to leave her home and her usual life behind on the basis that it allowed her to focus without distractions or phone interruptions.

During her time with Martin, they recorded a song titled 'Whataya Want From Me'. Although it didn't make the final track list for *Funhouse*, the song was given to Adam Lambert for his debut album. When Lambert's version became a successful single, Pink would release her original recording on her 2010 compilation album, *Greatest Hits... So Far!!!*

Pink initially wanted to name her album Heartbreak Is A Motherfucker, but her record label rejected the title due to concerns about offensive language affecting sales. Pink also didn't want the album to be perceived solely as a break-up album, even though it contained a lot of break-up themes. She explained, "There is a lot of that [break-up], but there is fun happening too, and that's why I named it *Funhouse* in the end."

Pink described life as a carnival, saying, "Clowns are supposed to be happy, but they are really scary. Carnivals are supposed to be fun, but really they are kind of creepy." She elaborated, "Love is supposed to be fun, but it can sometimes be really scary. And the funhouse mirrors that make you look so distorted that you don't recognise yourself, and you ask yourself, 'How did I get here? How do I get out of here?' But, you think that you want to do it again. That is the same as love and life. It's a metaphor for being in love and for life."

Pink said at the time that *Funhouse* was her most vulnerable and personal album yet. Much of the material reflected her separation from her husband. The first track, 'So What', starts with the line, "I guess I just lost my husband/I don't know where he went." 'Please Don't Leave Me' also explores the separation, where Pink sings of someone having a bad effect on her, yet her not being able to let go of them.

'So What' was co-written by Pink, Shellback (Karl Johan Schuster), and Max Martin. Martin also produced and recorded the song at Maratone Studios in Stockholm, Sweden. Additionally, Al Clay recorded parts of the song at the House of Blues Studio in Los Angeles, California. The song was mixed by Serban Ghenea at MixStar Studios in Virginia Beach, Virginia, with John Hanes handling the editing using Pro Tools technology, assisted by Tim Roberts. The final mastering was done by Tom Coyne at Sterling Sound in New York City.

The bold and unapologetic track has a catchy hook and an infectious energy that immediately grabs the listener's attention, making it a standout song that would surely resonate with fans who appreciate Pink's fearless approach to music. 'So What' is rooted in rock, with a strong pop sensibility that makes it instantly accessible and radio-friendly. The song opens with a punchy guitar riff that sets the tone for the rest of the track. The driving rhythm and upbeat tempo create a sense of urgency and excitement, propelling the song forward with relentless energy. Pink's vocal delivery is confident and assertive, reflecting the song's defiant lyrics and rebellious attitude.

Pink's vocal performance on 'So What' is a key element of the song's musical style. She brings an edgy quality to her singing, delivering the lyrics with a mix of attitude and playfulness. Her powerful voice cuts through the instrumentation, commanding attention and adding to the song's high-energy vibe.

Pink's vocal range and versatility are on full display, as she moves from melodic verses to anthemic choruses with ease. This vocal power adds depth and emotion to the song, reinforcing its message of resilience and empowerment. The song's catchy chorus and memorable hook make it a sing-along anthem, inviting listeners to join in and embrace their own rebellious side.

Despite its rebellious edge, 'So What' also has a sense of humour and playfulness, adding to its appeal. The song's lyrics contain witty and cheeky lines, delivered with a touch of sarcasm that showcases Pink's unique personality. This playful element adds a layer of charm to the song, making it enjoyable and relatable. The combination of rock-infused energy and playful humour creates a musical style that is both bold and fun, reflecting Pink's multifaceted approach to music.

The musical style of 'So What' would serve to make it a perfect fit for live performances. The song's high energy and anthemic quality would go on to translate well to the stage, allowing Pink to deliver dynamic and engaging performances, encouraging audience participation and interaction. This stage-friendly musical style would make 'So What' a staple in Pink's concert setlists, reinforcing its popularity and enduring appeal.

In 'Mean', Pink questions the breakdown of a relationship, singing, "It was good in the beginning/but how did we get so mean?" She co-wrote the song with Billy Mann, who had also collaborated with her on 'Stupid Girls', 'Dear Mr. President', and 'I'm Not Dead', among other tracks.

In 'It's All Your Fault', Pink blames her partner for raising her expectations of a romantic relationship and then giving up on her. The lyrics include lines like, "I conjure up the thought of being gone, but I'd probably even do that wrong." The song suggests that her partner's actions led her to question herself.

'Glitter In The Air' poses a series of reflective questions, such as, "Have you ever looked fear in the face and said I just don't care?" and "Have you ever hated yourself for staring at the phone?" Pink would go on to reveal that she doesn't have all the answers to the questions she asks in the song, acknowledging that she's still in the process of figuring things out.

Written by Pink, Nate "Danja" Hills, Kara DioGuardi, and Marcella Araica, with production by Danja, Kanal, and Jimmy Harry, 'Sober' was inspired by Pink's time at a party at her home where everyone was drunk except for her, and she felt like she wanted everyone to leave. She went to the beach, where she had a line in her head: "How do I feel so good sober?" Although the song's title might suggest it's about alcohol, Pink went on to explain that it's more about self-identity.

'Ave Mary A' addresses global issues and problems, while 'One Foot Wrong' describes an acid trip that went wrong, whilst also conveying a deeper theme. According to Pink, "That song is also about losing control and how easy it is to lose the plot in life and teeter on the edge."

The title track, 'Funhouse' reflects on a situation that once was enjoyable but no longer is. Pink noted, "It's about when the box you're in doesn't fit anymore, burn that fucker down and start a new one."

At the time, Pink cited her favourite track on the album as being 'Crystal Ball'. She mentioned that it was recorded in one take without any mixing, going straight to the master recording. Appreciating the candour and spontaneity of the song, she stated that it was "all about a vibe and not about perfection or being polished." She added, "I just love that song, and I loved recording it."

As the lead single from *Funhouse*, 'So What' was first released digitally in various countries on 11th August 2008. It began being played on US contemporary hit radio on 25th August. The song received positive reviews from music critics and became Pink's most successful single at the time, reaching number one in eleven countries, including the US, the UK, and Australia.

The music video for 'So What', directed by Dave Meyers, premiered on 22nd August, featuring a cameo by Carey Hart. Meyers, renowned for creating music videos with artists giving over-the-top portrayals of celebrities or themselves, had worked with Pink several times before, particularly on the music videos for 'U + Ur Hand' and 'Stupid Girls', both of which won MTV Video Music Awards for Best Pop Video. Besides these, Pink collaborated with Meyers on the music videos for 'There You Go', 'Most Girls', 'You Make Me Sick', 'Get The Party Started', 'Don't Let Me Get Me', and 'Feel Good Time'.

'So What' went on to be acclaimed as one of the best music videos of the year. When the single was nominated for Best Female Pop Vocal Performance at the fifty-first Grammy Awards, its music video received a nomination for Best Female Video at the 2009 MTV Video Music Awards. Clearly, Pink had fun filming it. She posted on her website: "If you EVER get a chance to drive a lawnmower down Sunset Blvd – I highly suggest it. Thanks for making my day. I'm really, really, really excited."

'Sober' was released as the second single from *Funhouse* on 10th November 2008. It became a commercial success, reaching the top ten in more than ten countries, including the UK, Canada, and Australia, and peaking at number fifteen on the Billboard Hot 100. The music video, directed by Jonas Åkerlund, premiered on 25th November on Pink's official YouTube channel. At the fifty-second Grammy Awards, it received a nomination in the same category that 'So What' had been in.

The third single, 'Please Don't Leave Me', was released in

January 2009 in Australia and in March 2009 in the US. It reached the top ten in several European countries, number eight in Canada, number twelve in the UK, and number seventeen in the US. The video, directed by Dave Meyers, drew inspiration from Stephen King-based films like *Misery*, along with other thrillers such as *Cujo*, *The Shining*, and *What Ever Happened To Baby Jane?* The video blends horror and thriller elements with a touch of dark comedy, which led to Pink releasing a censored version of it.

'Bad Influence' was released in Australia as the fourth single to promote the start of the Australian leg of the Funhouse Tour. It was made available as a CD and digital single in May 2009. Despite lacking a music video, the song achieved significant success in Oceania, reaching the top ten in both Australia and New Zealand. It was later released in Germany on 26th March 2010, where it reached number twenty-six on the official singles chart and topped the national airplay chart. In April 2011, 'Bad Influence' was released in the Netherlands to promote Pink's compilation album, *Greatest Hits... So Far!!!*

'Funhouse' was released digitally in the US on 2nd July 2009 as the fifth single from the album. In the UK, the music video premiered on 20th June 2009 on *4Music*, featuring Tony Kanal of No Doubt, the co-writer and producer of the song, playing the piano. 'Funhouse' had a moderate chart performance, reaching number forty-four on the Billboard Hot 100.

'I Don't Believe You', the sixth single, was released in the US on 5th October 2009, but did not chart on the Billboard Hot 100.

'Glitter In The Air' was quickly sent to radio as a new single by Jive Records after Pink had performed it at the fifty-second Grammy Awards – before the broadcast had even finished! On the 20th February 2010, the song debuted on the Billboard Hot 100 at number eighteen. The seventh single from *Funhouse*, it helped to boost the album's sales and push it back into the top twenty on the Billboard 200 chart. The live audio recording of Pink's Grammy performance was released digitally on 1st February 2010.

'Ave Mary A' was released as a single in Australia in 2010, peaking at number ten on the Australian Airplay Chart. Despite being the twenty-fourth most played song on Australian radio in 2010, it did not place on the ARIA singles chart.

Evidently, a remarkable number of songs from *Funhouse* were released as singles. This approach demonstrates that there was a substantial market for Pink's music, highlighting her enduring popularity and versatility as an artist. Also, the release of multiple singles from the album plausibly served to keep people interested in *Funhouse*, and Pink overall; it enabled her to maintain a consistent presence on the airwaves, in music charts, and across media platforms.

Funhouse itself, released in October 2008, was met with predominantly positive reviews from music critics. It debuted at number two on the Billboard 200 chart, selling 180,000 copies in its first week, and reached the top spot in seven countries, including Australia, New Zealand, the Netherlands, Ireland, and the UK. *Funhouse* became Pink's first number one album in the UK, entering at number one on 2nd November 2008. It would go on to be certified four times Platinum by the British Phonographic Industry for selling over 1.2 million copies. Notably in the UK, it became the ninth-biggest selling record of 2008, and the twenty-third-biggest seller of 2009.

Overall, *Funhouse* peaked within the top ten in over twenty countries. It earned double-platinum certification from the Recording Industry Association of America and thirteen times platinum from the Australian Recording Industry Association.

Sydney's *Daily Telegraph* opined; "The record is a balanced blend of upbeat pop gems and mid-tempo ballads... The power of Pink's pop lies in the clever juxtaposition of heartfelt honesty about her life with anthematic choruses and irresistible melodies tailor-made to be screamed out by her fans."

Indeed, such was Australia's enthusiasm for *Funhouse* that record shops broke the official release date embargo and put the album on sale the day before its official release date. That one day of sales alone ensured it was the fourth-highest-selling album of the week, shifting 7,120 copies.

The Funhouse Tour dates for Europe, Australia, and North America were announced in early 2009. The first leg of the tour covered Europe, followed by a three-month run in Australia. The third leg took place in North America, including eleven dates in the US and one in Canada. The fourth leg was three months long, starting on 14th October in Dublin, Ireland, and concluding on 20th December in Hannover, Germany.

Pink broke records in Australia during the tour, selling out seventeen shows in Melbourne (more than any other city), making it the city with the most tickets sold and the highest revenue. In Sydney, Pink sold out seven consecutive shows in a single week, with all tickets purchased within forty minutes.

This high demand allowed Pink to surpass her record-breaking run of thirty-five sold-out shows from the 2007 Australian leg of the I'm Not Dead Tour. The Funhouse Tour completed fifty-eight shows in Australia, establishing Pink as the most successful touring artist in the country's history. Additional records broken during the tour included the most shows at the Sydney Entertainment Centre and the Brisbane Entertainment Centre.

The US tour dates marked Pink's first tour in her home country since 2006. The tour's US leg began in Seattle in September 2009 and concluded in New York City after twelve shows.

With the release of the album's Tour Edition, a live album featuring twelve performances was also released, along with 'Push You Away', a previously unreleased studio track included in the Tour Edition. The accompanying DVD contains twenty-three live performances with two bonus performances. A Blu-ray version of the DVD was also made available. These recordings took place in Sydney, Australia, on 17th and 18th July 2009.

A year later, in 2010, Pink embarked on the Funhouse Summer Carnival Tour across Europe. The tour was announced by promoter Eventim on 14th October 2009, followed by a November announcement on Pink's official website. After selling over two-million tickets on her successful Funhouse Tour, it was announced that the Grammy Award-winning singer-songwriter would embark on her first-ever stadium tour of Europe.

In December 2009, it was also confirmed that Pink would headline various music festivals throughout Europe during the tour. During an interview with online radio station IN:DEMAND, Pink mentioned that the new tour would have a different setlist and fewer acrobatics, confirming that it wasn't just a continuation of her previous tour.

Even with less acrobatic demands, the tour wouldn't be a

breeze. The Funhouse Summer Carnival Tour was scheduled to start on 27th May 2010, at the Expo-Gelände in Hanover, Germany, but this show was cancelled due to logistical issues. Then, on 15th July 2010, during a show in Nuremberg, Germany, Pink was injured while performing 'So What'; her left-side flywire was activated before the right-side one was properly attached to her harness. This caused her to be pulled off the stage and onto a barricade below, just before she was about to perform an aerial acrobatic routine. The song was stopped, and she was rushed to the hospital. Later, she tweeted that she hadn't suffered any broken bones or serious injuries. The stunt was temporarily removed from the show, but it returned on 20th July during the concert in Prague, Czech Republic, where Pink successfully soared through the crowd in her harness.

Certainly, turbulences both major and minor couldn't put a stop to Pink's success during the *Funhouse* period of her career. After reuniting with Hart in January 2009, Pink mentioned on *The Ellen DeGeneres Show* that she found it funny to perform 'So What' when he was in the audience, especially the part where she sang the lyric, 'you're a tool.'

Although Pink's separation from her husband had served as strong inspiration for 'So What' and indeed much of the emotional element of *Funhouse* overall, everything worked out well for her in the end. Not only did the album achieve significant success, but the personal struggles that influenced its creation became a source of strength. Pink's journey from separation to reconciliation demonstrated her resilience and ability to overcome adversity. The success of *Funhouse* and her renewed relationship with her husband brought a sense of closure and a happy ending to this chapter in Pink's life.

CHAPTER EIGHT
AN ALL-STAR LINE-UP

In November 2010, Pink released her first greatest hits album, *Greatest Hits... So Far!!!* The album produced two singles, 'Raise Your Glass' and 'Fuckin' Perfect', both of which were met with considerable success.

'Raise Your Glass' was co-written with Max Martin and Shellback, and produced by Martin and Schuster. The song is a celebration of the first decade since Pink's debut in 2000, and it is dedicated to her fans who have supported her throughout the years. It follows a strong pop style, similar to Pink's previous work with Martin. She described the song as a "celebration for people who feel left out from the popular crowd."

In an interview with MTV, Pink commented on the song's inspiration and purpose: "I don't know if it's going to be huge, but it is new. I did three new songs. It was good timing. I had been on the road for two years and I hadn't written anything, and I wanted to write a song about underdogs. Instead of becoming a cover girl, I hit the road and pounded the pavement... and became a touring artist. You don't have to be popular when you're a touring artist, you just have to be good. This is a thank you to the fans."

Released on 5th October 2010 on Jive Records, 'Raise Your Glass' achieved both critical and commercial success, with most music critics praising it and describing it as a party anthem. It hit the top ten in several countries, including the US. It got to number thirteen in the UK, and to number one in Australia.

'Fuckin' Perfect' (stylised as 'Perfect' on the clean version and as 'F**kin' Perfect' on the main cover) was also a collaboration with Max Martin and Shellback. The track is a power ballad encouraging people to embrace their authentic selves and accept one another for who they truly are. The song was released on 14th December 2010 by Jive Records.

Pink said that Carey Hart was the main inspiration for 'Fuckin' Perfect.' The music video, directed by longtime collaborator Dave Meyers, sends a message against depression, self-harm, and suicide. In November 2011, the song received a Grammy Award nomination for Best Pop Solo Performance.

'Fuckin' Perfect' reached number two on the Billboard Hot 100. It also peaked at number two in Canada, Hungary, New Zealand, and Poland.

The music video for 'Fuckin' Perfect' was filmed on 5th December 2010, during Pink's early weeks of pregnancy. The video centres on the life of a woman who overcame numerous challenges to become a successful artist. The lead role was portrayed by Tina Majorino, who Pink described on Twitter and Facebook as "insanely talented."

Billboard described the video as "controversial," saying, "Choosing to title her new single 'Fuckin' Perfect' and then open its video with graphic depictions of sex and bloody scenarios of cutting and suicide, Pink knew her latest project would ignite controversy. And that's just the way she wants it, because in this particular case, the thirty-one-year-old singer's in-your-face approach is to ensure the message in the music isn't lost or ignored."

Indeed, by addressing the subject of mental health without reservation or apology, Pink once again succeeded to create a safe space through her music, empowering listeners to explore their feelings and acknowledge their struggles. As a prominent figure in the music industry, Pink's willingness to address mental health in her music has made her an inspirational role model for fans of all ages. Her openness and honesty has the scope to resonate with listeners who have felt isolated or misunderstood, providing a sense of solidarity and hope.

Pink's philanthropy would also shine brightly during this period of her career. She sang on the 2010 remake of the charity single, 'We Are The World.' She also collaborated on Herbie Hancock's album, *The Imagine Project*, where she sang Peter Gabriel's 'Don't Give Up' with John Legend and contributed vocals to John Lennon's 'Imagine' alongside Seal, India Arie, Jeff Beck, Konono N°1, Oumou Sangaré, and others. Hancock described the project as "an effort to show the power and beauty of global collaboration as a path to peace." The collaboration earned Pink a Grammy Award for Best Pop Collaboration with Vocals.

On 2nd June 2011, Pink welcomed her first child, a daughter – Willow Sage Hart. Although there was speculation in the media that Pink might take a long break from music to focus on motherhood, her management team mentioned in an interview with *American Top 40* that she could release a new album the following year.

And albums aside, Pink provided the voice for the character Gloria in the animated film *Happy Feet Two*, which premiered in the US on 18th November 2011. In addition to her voice acting role, she sang the movie's theme song, 'Bridge Of Light.'

In March 2012, Pink announced on Twitter that she had started working on her sixth studio album. In an open letter to her fans on her official website, she described the process of creating the album, saying, "I'm putting my heart and soul into every song, and there's a lot of that these days. This little girl has expanded me and what I am capable of feeling as a human."

Pink later appeared on the cover of *Cosmopolitan* in June 2012. During her interview, she spoke about her return to the music scene, indicating that the new album would be released in the fall of the same year. She mentioned that she collaborated with Billy Mann and others on the new music. Pink said, "I've been in mommy mode, and I'm just starting to get back out there into the real world. I've been in the studio recording my new album, so now it feels like everything is falling back into place."

The development of Pink's sixth album, *The Truth About Love*, occurred between January and May 2012. Recording sessions took place at various studios, including Earthstar Creation Centre in Venice, Conway Recording Studios in Los Angeles, Suite 203, and The Modern Dirt Laboratories in London.

Before starting work on the album, Pink considered how to balance her music career with motherhood. In an interview with *Rolling Stone*, she shared, "Every album, I'm worried that I'm a dork and a fraud – what if I can't sing anymore? Then I stop thinking and start playing guitar, and I realise that it's okay to suck and move forward."

While her earlier albums involved late-night recording sessions, Pink said that becoming a mother changed her approach to making music, leading to a more structured routine. Recording sessions for *The Truth About Love* were scheduled from Monday to Friday, between 1pm and 10pm, with breaks for dinner and nursing her daughter. Weekend days were taken as time off, reserved for family.

For *The Truth About Love*, Pink enlisted the support of her longtime collaborators Billy Mann, Butch Walker, and Max Martin, and also worked with new collaborators Jeff Bhasker and Dan Wilson. Pink would go on to mention that she began work on the album as "an experiment," meeting with Mann first because she felt secure in what she called a "no-shame zone."

She also reunited with record producer Greg Kurstin, with whom she hadn't worked since her fourth studio album, *I'm Not Dead*. Valuing her connection with Kurstin, Pink believed that he would understand her musical direction and enhance her production and musicality.

Around forty songs were written during the album's development. Pink mentioned that she would write ideas for songs in her journal. The title track was the song that helped her recognise that the album was forming a cohesive theme around the concept of love.

Pink's songwriting around this time was inspired by the array of emotions she had experienced during her "exhausting search" for love and the year she and her husband Carey Hart were separated. Admitting that she was "still exorcising some demons" when explaining her approach to songwriting, Pink would go on to tell the *Daily News* that the album reflected her life at the time and her newfound happiness, which had been influenced by her becoming a mother. She noted that "It's just a lot more fun... I think that's a new thing for me."

Pink also aimed to enhance the musicality of the album and set a higher standard for herself, taking a greater interest in the production aspects. Producer Greg Kurstin mentioned that Pink's creative process was fluid, noting that she would compose lyrics quickly once inspired, likening her work ethic to a stream of consciousness. Each day in the studio resulted in a new completed song, with Pink typically recording just "one or two takes," which Kurstin said were "usually amazing."

Every song on *The Truth About Love* was co-written by Pink, except for 'Try', which was written by Michael Busbee and Ben West. This track was originally recorded in 2010 by their former band, GoNorthToGoSouth.

Busbee and West had initially pitched 'Try' to Rani Hancock, an A&R executive at RCA Records, hoping to give the song to Kelly Clarkson or Daughtry. A demo version was also recorded by Adam Lambert, but according to Busbee, it "just wasn't the right fit." The song was later played at a label meeting, and then pitched to Pink, who agreed to record it. Busbee would go on to note that it was one of the first outside songs Pink had recorded in a long time.

The concept for 'Just Give Me A Reason' emerged during a songwriting session with Jeff Bhasker and Nate Ruess. Bhasker was introduced to Pink by Peter Edge, an executive at RCA Records. Pink approached Ruess because she was intrigued by his "intense incredible" voice.

After the first verse had been written, Pink continued to work on the lyrics at home. She felt that the song's conversational style required another vocalist, so she chose Ruess to sing the duet with her. However, Ruess was hesitant to record the song as a duet since he had only recorded a demo. Despite this, Pink eventually persuaded him to join her on it after "many, many months of convincing." She went on to remark that she had "totally tricked him into doing it," adding that no one could have done it better. She also believed that Ruess was happy that he'd done it.

A pop album that also incorporates elements of electropop, dance-pop, and rock music, *The Truth About Love* primarily consists of energetic pop songs with catchy hooks and confessional power ballads. The album's instrumentation includes dance beats, rock guitars, piano melodies, string orchestras, and hip-hop loops. Pink would describe the album as a personal rock record focused on monogamous relationships and various perspectives on love – touching on its light and dark aspects, the joy it brings, and the pain it can cause.

The lyrical themes also include topics of sex, self-reliance, long-term relationships, and rebellion – all of which Pink had explored on previous albums. However, *The Truth About Love* marks a shift in her vocal style; she had quit smoking, which had resulted in her being able to expand her upper vocal range by an octave.

The album begins with 'Are We All We Are', a self-empowering protest song with crashing drums, keyboards, and disorientated synthesisers. The lyrics are influenced by economic inequality.

In 2011, the Occupy Wall Street Movement, often abbreviated as 'OWS', had emerged as a social and political movement in New York City. It quickly spread to other cities around the world. The movement aimed to draw attention to economic inequality, corporate greed, and the influence of money in politics.

Participants in the Occupy movement protested against the disproportionate concentration of wealth among the top one percent of income earners and advocated for greater economic justice and social change. The movement's relevance to contemporary culture was significant, sparking discussions about income inequality and challenging the status quo in corporate and financial practices.

The influence of the Occupy Wall Street Movement in the lyrics of 'Are We All We Are' is evident, and an impressive example of how Pink uses her music to raise awareness about the issues that the movement brought to the forefront.

'Blow Me (One Last Kiss)' is an energetic electropop song that can be aptly described as a break-up anthem. With its driving beat, rock riffs, and snappy guitars, and its bold and defiant vibe, the song has drawn comparisons to Kelly Clarkson's 'Stronger (What Doesn't Kill You).'

The latter is a similar break-up anthem with a high-energy feel. The resemblance between the two songs can be attributed to their shared producer, Greg Kurstin, as well as the rock-influenced sound and themes of resilience that they both embody.

Both songs focus on themes of empowerment, with the break-up anthem serving as a rallying cry for personal strength and independence. In 'Blow Me (One Last Kiss)', Pink sings about leaving behind a toxic relationship with a sense of defiance and self-assurance. Similarly, in 'Stronger (What Doesn't Kill You),' Kelly Clarkson's lyrics emphasise the idea that adversity can lead to growth and inner strength.

'Try' is a power ballad with a 1980s vibe that explores a damaged relationship and the risks of love. It is followed by 'Just Give Me A Reason.' A duet with Nate Ruess, the lyrics depict Pink pleading with a partner as they work to keep their relationship together.

'True Love' is a humorous ska-pop and pop-rock song featuring guest vocals from Lily Allen. The lyrics are something of a celebration of dysfunctional love, recounting aspects of Pink's turbulent relationship. In this ballad, Pink and Allen each sing a verse before joining together on the chorus.

By partnering with Allen, Pink was able to tap into a new fan base and attract listeners who appreciate Allen's unique sound and attitude. This cross-pollination of fan bases may have served to increase album sales and streaming numbers, enticing fans of both artists to explore the collaborative track.

With collaborations tending to be a good idea due to how they can generate buzz and media attention, further boosting an album's visibility and commercial appeal, it was also the case that Allen brought an interesting vocal contrast to 'True Love.'

Known for her distinctive style, characterised by witty lyrics and a blend of pop and indie influences, Lily Allen complemented Pink's bold and edgy approach to the track. The combination of their voices and musical sensibilities offers a compelling contrast that adds depth to *The Truth About Love* overall.

This partnership presented Pink with the opportunity to explore different sonic landscapes and incorporate new influences, enhancing the album's overall diversity; their combined talents and distinctive styles created a dynamic that added an extra layer of interest to the album.

A beneficial experience for Lily Allen, her participation on 'True Love' marked her first track since she had announced her return to the pop scene in 2012. Prior to that, she had retired in 2009 to focus on parenthood, her record label, and her fashion boutique.

'How Come You're Not Here?' is a 1970s-inspired glam rock and blues number that showcases Pink's furious side. With lyrics about when a partner might be involved with someone else, the song has distorted vocals, layered guitars, and bells played by Pink's daughter Willow.

The inclusion of Willow's bell-playing on *The Truth About Love* is demonstrative of a personal and heartfelt connection between Pink's music and her family life. It shows Pink's commitment to incorporating her role as a mother into her artistic endeavours, bridging the gap between personal and professional. The bells, though a small element, showcases the human side of music production, reminding fans that even in the midst of creating a chart-topping album, Pink is also a loving mother who cherishes her family.

'Slut Like You' is an electroclash track with tongue-in-cheek lyrics that focus on female empowerment and embracing one's sexuality. Critics would go on to note similarities between this track and Blur's 1997 single, 'Song 2'.

One of the key similarities between 'Slut Like You' and 'Song 2' is the high-energy vibe that drives both tracks. 'Slut Like You' features pulsating electronic beats and powerful guitar riffs, creating a sense of urgency and excitement. Similarly, 'Song 2' is known for its explosive guitar sound and iconic "Woo-hoo!" chorus, which captures a raw and intense energy. This shared high-octane feel contributes to the comparison, as both tracks are designed to get listeners moving and create a lively atmosphere.

Another similarity between the two tracks are their rock influences and dynamic song structures. 'Slut Like You' incorporates elements of rock, with crunchy guitar riffs and a driving rhythm that complements its electroclash foundation. The song's dynamic structure, with its shifts in tempo and intensity, adds to its appeal. 'Song 2' also incorporates rock elements, with distorted guitars and a strong backbeat that create a powerful, energetic sound. Both tracks use these rock influences to add depth and complexity, resulting in an engaging and energetic listening experience.

The title track, 'The Truth About Love', has something of a retro 1960s style to it. It explores the complexities of a long-term relationship and the realities that come with it.

An acoustic ballad, 'Beam Me Up' reflects on taking a break from reality and longing to be with someone who has died. Pink would go on to share that the song was written "through a lot of tears" and was inspired by a close friend whose child had passed away.

'Walk Of Shame' is an anthemic new wave style song about the embarrassment and regret experienced the morning after a one-night stand.

'Here Comes The Weekend' includes dance elements, and features guest vocals from Eminem. The song is about letting loose at a party. Known for his rapid-fire rapping and edgy lyrical style, Eminem, like Lily Allen, brought a unique energy to *The Truth About Love*, complementing Pink's powerful vocals and fearless attitude.

Another high-profile collaboration on the album, it would serve to contribute to its success by attracting attention and adding a dynamic contrast to the musical mix. Eminem's reputation as one of the most successful and controversial rappers of all time would ensure that his involvement would generate buzz and attract a large audience.

Pink explained how they arranged the collaboration: "He said, 'Do you want to do a song with me?' 'Fuck yeah!' I said, 'Do you want to do a song with me?' and he said, 'Fuck yeah!' Handshake. Nothing signed. Done." (Pink had also featured on 'Won't Back Down' on Eminem's 2010 album, *Recovery*, with Eminem having chosen her because he believed she would do justice to the song).

The following track, 'Where Did The Beat Go?', is a mid-tempo R&B song with military drums and multi-layered vocals. Its lyrics reveal a vulnerable Pink questioning a relationship that seems to be falling apart and feeling as if she is no longer desired.

The final song on the standard edition of the album, 'The Great Escape', is a piano ballad with sombre lyrics that explores themes of medication, enduring challenging times, and contemplating suicide.

The deluxe version includes 'My Signature Move', an anthemic pop-rock song produced by Butch Walker. 'Is This Thing On?' features a typical disco rhythm in which the bass drum hits on every beat.

With heartfelt lyrics, 'Run' is an emotional power ballad dedicated to Pink's daughter. In its exploration of the profound bond between mother and child, it expresses a love that is both protective and unconditional. The song's emotional depth and poignant themes make it a standout piece, resonating with listeners who appreciate Pink's ability to convey the complexities of parenthood through her music.

The final track on the deluxe edition, 'Good Old Days', carries a live-in-the-moment message, along with melancholic lyrics.

Serving to build excitement and anticipation for Pink's fans, the cover artwork for *The Truth About Love* was revealed on her official website on 16th July 2012. Photographed by Andrew Macpherson, the cover shows Pink with her signature pink hair, crouching down while wearing a short black top, short black shorts, garters, and red heels. Pink had revealed the title of her new album during an interview on Australia's *Today* show on 4th July 2012. The day after that, she confirmed that the album would be released on 17th September 2012 in the UK, and on 18th September 2012 in the US.

In 2011, RCA Music Group had announced that it would be disbanding Jive Records, Arista, and J Records. As a result, all artists previously signed to those labels, including Pink, would release their future material through RCA Records.

On 4th September 2012, Pink announced a partnership with the American retail company Target for a promotional campaign. The partnership involved releasing the exclusive deluxe edition of *The Truth About Love* with the four extra tracks, along with Pink appearing in Target television commercials to promote the album.

A special fan edition of the album was released in November 2012. This edition, in addition to the standard album, contains six additional songs, as well as a DVD featuring music videos for 'Blow Me (One Last Kiss)' and 'Try', four live performances from a special *The Truth About Love* concert in Los Angeles, and behind-the-scenes footage from the album's photo shoot.

The Truth About Love was met with generally favourable reviews. *Entertainment Weekly* commended the confessional nature of the songs, describing the album as "honesty you can dance to." *The Guardian* noted that Pink "funnels her thoughts into some of the most pungent songs in pop" and applauded her for having "the nous to convert raw emotion into pop-punk earworms."

Spin compared the album favourably to Kelly Clarkson's *Stronger* (2011), stating that both records "are stocked with confidence-jolting up-tempo jams, broken-hearted weepers, and candid explorations of their own flaws." The publication also remarked that both singers "have dug in their heels even harder for guitar pop," as opposed to following current musical trends.

Indeed, by this point in her career, thanks to her established reputation and solid fan base, Pink was in a good place to take musical risks. She was in a relative position of freedom to explore new musical territories without feeling pressured to stick to genres with a proven commercial edge. This allowed her the opportunity to defy expectations in a way that might have been riskier for a less-established artist.

The Truth About Love became Pink's first number one album in the US, debuting at the top of the Billboard 200 chart with 280,000 copies sold, her biggest first-week sales at that time. The following week, the album dropped to number four, selling 94,000 copies.

By the end of 2012, it had sold 945,000 copies, making it the twelfth-highest-selling album in the US for that year. By December 2013, sales had exceeded 1.83 million copies. The album would go on to receive a three times Platinum certification from the Recording Industry Association of America (RIAA) in August 2017, representing over three-million album-equivalent units sold in the US.

The Truth About Love debuted at number two on the UK albums chart, selling 80,000 copies in its first week. It was just behind The Killers' *Battle Born*, which sold 94,000 copies. By February 2019, the album would go on to receive a three times Platinum certification from the British Phonographic Industry (BPI) for 907,000 copies sold.

In Australia, *The Truth About Love* debuted at number one on the ARIA Albums Chart, with first-week sales of 74,293 copies, becoming Pink's fourth number one album in the country and achieving the biggest single-week sales of 2012. The album stayed at the top of the chart for ten non-consecutive weeks, marking the longest-running number one album since Adele's *21* in 2011. *The Truth About Love* was Australia's best-selling album in two consecutive years (2012 and 2013). It was the first album to achieve this.

By January 2014, the album had gone on to sell 560,000 copies in Australia and was certified nine times Platinum by the Australian Recording Industry Association (ARIA), representing sales of over 630,000 units. The album saw similar success in New Zealand, debuting at the top of the Official New Zealand Music Chart and spending six non-consecutive weeks there. It earned a four times Platinum certification from Recorded Music NZ (RMNZ) for shipments exceeding 60,000 units.

In Canada, *The Truth About Love* debuted at the top of the Canadian Albums Chart, with 28,000 copies sold in its first week, becoming Pink's first number one album in Canada. It was certified three times Platinum by Music Canada for shipments of 240,000 copies.

In France, the album debuted at number four on the official album chart, with 17,855 traditional units sold. It earned a Platinum certification from the Syndicat National de l'Édition Phonographique (SNAP), indicating sales of 100,000 copies.

The Truth About Love reached number one on album charts in Austria, Germany, Sweden, and Switzerland. It also placed within the top ten in several other countries, including Denmark, Italy, the Netherlands, and Spain.

Impressively, on a global basis, *The Truth About Love* was the seventh-best-selling album of 2012, with sales of 2.6 million copies. By November 2016, it had gone on to sell an estimated seven-million copies worldwide.

Billboard would go on to rank *The Truth About Love* as one of the best albums of the 2010s decade, praising Pink for creating a "ramshackle masterpiece" that explores the complexities of being human by integrating her experiences as a family woman into her music.

The album was nominated for Best Pop Vocal Album at the

fifty-fifth Annual Grammy Awards, while 'Just Give Me A Reason' received nominations for Song of the Year and Best Pop Duo/Group Performance at the fifty-sixth Grammy Awards. In Canada, the album was nominated for International Album of the Year at the 2014 Juno Awards.

The lead single from the album, 'Blow Me (One Last Kiss)', was released on 2nd July 2012, a week earlier than planned due to a demo having been leaked online. The song received positive reviews from music critics, who praised Pink's vocals and the song's anthemic chorus, considering it a return to form for the singer. The single reached the top of the charts in Australia and Hungary and peaked at number five on the Billboard Hot 100. The accompanying music video, directed by Dave Meyers, was released on 26th July 2012. It portrays Pink taking revenge by crashing the wedding of a former lover.

'Try' was released as the second single from *The Truth About Love* on 6th September 2012. The song achieved top ten status in the US and in fifteen other countries, including the UK, Australia, Canada, and Germany. The music video was directed by Floria Sigismondi and choreographed by the Golden Boyz and Sebastien Stella. It features Pink and her lover, played by Colt Prattes, engaging in an intense love story and expressing their frustrations through intricate choreography, inspired by the Apache dance. "Making this video was the most fun I've ever had in my entire career," said Pink. "I never wanted it to end. It's my favourite video ever."

'Just Give Me A Reason' was released as the third single from the album on 26th February 2013. The song achieved significant commercial success, reaching the top of the charts in over ten countries and landing in the top ten in others. In the US, it spent three consecutive weeks at number one. The accompanying music video, directed by Diane Martel, primarily takes place on a floating mattress surrounded by mist and water, featuring a cameo from Carey Hart.

The fourth single from the album, 'True Love', was released on 28th June 2013. The song achieved moderate success, reaching the top forty in over fifteen countries, including Australia and Canada. The music video, released on 1st July 2013, shows Pink playing, fighting, and riding bicycles with her family, interspersed with clips from her tour performances.

'Walk Of Shame' was sent to Australian contemporary hit radio stations on 25th September 2013, as the fifth single from the album. Its music video features a compilation of concert and behind-the-scenes footage from The Truth About Love Tour.

In Europe, 'Are We All We Are' was released as the final single from the album on 31st October 2013.

As well as being supported by an abundance of single releases, accompanying videos and public appearances, *The Truth About Love* was further promoted through The Truth About Love Tour, which began on 13th February 2013, in Phoenix, Arizona. The first leg comprised twenty-six dates across North America. The second leg included thirty concerts throughout Europe. The third leg, from June to September, had forty-six dates in Australia. Pink then performed an additional forty shows in North America, starting on 10th October 2013, and ending on 31st January 2014.

For The Truth About Love Tour, a significant logistical effort was required, including a chartered 747 jumbo jet, nineteen semi-trailers, and a crew of eighty to transport and set up 400 tons of equipment.

The Truth About Love Tour set two records at the Rod Laver Arena in Melbourne, Australia. Pink holds the record for the most shows at the venue, with eighteen sold-out performances during The Truth About Love Tour, surpassing her previous record of seventeen shows during the 2009 Funhouse Tour. She also became the first artist to sell more than 250,000 tickets at the venue. On 26th August 2013, Pink was honoured with a plaque backstage, a second pink pole, a star at the venue's entrance, and Door 18 was painted pink.

Incredibly, Pink broke "local girl" Kylie Minogue's record for the most concerts by a female performer at the Entertainment Centre, with a total of twenty-six shows at the venue. In Sydney, her four sold-out shows at the Allphones Arena, where she sold over 67,000 tickets, surpassed the record set by Britney Spears in 2009 during her Circus Tour.

In Perth, after performing for nearly 15,000 fans per night, Pink also set the record for most performances by an artist at the

RAC Arena, as well as achieving the top four attended events at the venue.

President and CEO of Live Nation Australia, Michael Coppel, thanked Pink for spending three months on tour in the country: "Everyone at LNA has been thrilled to be involved in Pink's record-breaking tour, continuing a decade-long association with an artist who continues to set new standards and who has now sold in excess of 1.5 million tickets in Australia."

The combined gross from her Melbourne shows was 29.2 million US dollars, making it the largest gross for any headliner at a single venue in 2013.

Additionally, Pink sold out the KFC Yum! Centre, becoming the highest-grossing female artist to play at the arena to date.

Overall, across all locations visited, the entire tour became the third highest-grossing tour of 2013, earning a total of 183 million dollars with over 1.9 million tickets sold. A video album of the tour was released on 15th November 2013, in DVD, Blu-ray, and digital download formats.

As the third highest-grossing tour of 2013, The Truth About Love Tour was beaten only by Bon Jovi, and Cirque du Soleil's Michael Jackson The Immortal World Tour. Also that year, Pink emerged as the third-highest grossing female touring artist, beaten by only Beyoncé and Taylor Swift.

Unsurprisingly, perhaps, the tour garnered many positive reviews, with critics praising Pink's vocal performance, stage presence, and aerial acrobatics.

San Jose's *Mercury News* said Pink "is the new gold standard," adding; "You definitely don't walk away from a Pink show shrugging your shoulders and muttering 'meh.' It's far more likely that fans practically skip out of the building, feeling extremely satisfied with the experience and determined to tell others to 'go see Pink next time she's in town'... Honesty is, as they say, the best policy. And, after watching the Truth About Love Tour, I can honestly say that few, if any, performers deliver better pop spectacles than Pink."

The *Los Angeles Times* opined that Pink is: "perhaps the most gifted and imaginative physical performer in pop right now."

Rolling Stone described a performance as a "grown-up

sophisticated show," adding that "Pink was relaxed and chatty between songs." The publication also went on to elaborate that "by the time Pink was soaring gracefully through the air on cables stretched across the arena to perform 'So What', the singer had demonstrated an epic workout of vocals, stagecraft and stunt-work without missing a note. The night's best special effect was Pink herself."

Proving herself to be a versatile artist capable of doing justice to songs originally sung by other established artists, Pink was given praise by *The Australian*; "[Pink's] fearlessness was echoed with her first performance of Cyndi Lauper's 'Time After Time'. She tackled the pop classic with the lyrics in her hand, the tentative reading providing great balance with the precision required for most of the numbers. That may be Pink's greatest asset, that she can create a spectacular show that more than matches her peers, but the glitz never hides the pure, unvarnished talent at her core."

During this period of her career, besides her work on *The Truth About Love*, Pink collaborated on 'Guns And Roses' for T.I.'s album, *Trouble Man: Heavy Is The Head*. This track achieved Gold certification from ARIA, signifying 35,000 digital downloads in Australia.

Additionally, Pink contributed to Cher's album – *Closer To The Truth* – by writing two songs: 'I Walk Alone' and 'Lie To Me'. Pink also played a role in the 2012 film, *Thanks For Sharing*, alongside Gwyneth Paltrow and Mark Ruffalo. She portrayed a sex addict named Dede, earning critical acclaim for her performance. The movie premiered in the US on 20th September 2013, with Pink credited under her name Alecia Moore.

The Truth About Love period of Pink's career was a major success, marked by a chart-topping album with diverse collaborations, an embracement of motherhood and personal themes, and a record-breaking tour. These achievements kept Pink's commercial and artistic star burning bright, reinforcing her position as a leading figure in her field.

CHAPTER NINE
A PLEASANT DIVERSION

In 2014, Pink would take something of a diversion from her typical pop rock style to work on *Rose Ave*. The album, created in collaboration with Dallas Green under the moniker You+Me, saw Pink exploring a softer, folk-influenced sound that contrasted with the high-energy pop anthems for which she had become known. The project allowed her to showcase a different side of her musicality, demonstrating her versatility as an artist and her willingness to venture into other genres.

Pink and Green had been considering a collaboration for several years. They had met through mutual friends. Dallas Green recalled that Pink came to one of his shows in Los Angeles, and her husband, Carey Hart, already knew him.

Indeed, Pink had first become aware of Green's work when her husband played her his music. Pink was so impressed by it that she even listened to it while giving birth to Willow. "I don't remember what song it was," she told *The Guardian*. "I was high as shit on painkillers. But I've always been drawn to voices that make you feel one sound deeply. My favourite instrument is the violin, because no other instrument draws out the pain and the aching that's inside of me like it does. And Dallas' voice is like that violin."

In March 2014, Pink and Green were delighted to discover that their schedules finally aligned, allowing them to work together. The initial plan was to explore possibilities without necessarily committing to producing an album.

Both artists had prepared some material in advance, and Pink booked a studio as a precaution. Although Green had been unsure as to whether their voices would mesh, he found that their tones complemented each other, creating a harmonious balance (he would later go on to admit he was initially terrified to collaborate, but found that singing with Pink made him a better singer). Consequently, the pair spent a full week in the studio, writing and recording without the knowledge of their record labels. Almost the entire album was recorded within that week.

Both artists would go on to note that the absence of typical production pressures made the experience enjoyable and fulfilling. Green mentioned that the album felt very personal to both of them, while Pink expressed that the lack of expectations made the process a liberating experience saying, "I just felt like I was doing it because I loved it."

Every song on the album was written and produced by Pink and Green, except for 'No Ordinary Love,' which is a song by Sade, the band who had a 1984 hit with 'Smooth Operator.'

The musical style present on *Rose Ave.* is rooted in folk and acoustic elements, with harmonious vocals and organic instrumentation creating an intimate and contemplative atmosphere. The lyrical themes focus on love, relationships, personal growth, and reflections on the human condition, offering a poignant and introspective experience. The album's sense of intimacy and vulnerability, combined with its focus on universal themes, makes it a distinctive and rewarding project that showcases the depth and versatility of Pink and Dallas Green.

The album's arrangements are minimalistic yet rich, with acoustic guitars, piano, and subtle percussion providing a warm and organic backdrop. This stripped-down approach creates a sense of pleasant simplicity, allowing the vocals and lyrics to take centre stage.

The interplay between the two distinctively different voices creates a beautiful blend of tones, with Pink's powerful vocals balancing Green's softer, mellower style. This vocal harmony is central to the album's appeal, evoking a sense of connection and unity. The acoustic duets give the songs a raw and authentic quality, emphasising the emotional depth of the lyrics.

Evidently, Pink's foray into a more acoustic sound wasn't something she considered to be an exception. "In the same concerts where I'm flying around, I'm always barefoot and sitting with an acoustic guitar too," she told *The Guardian*. "In every show, I do an acoustic section, so it's a very big part of me."

Songs like 'Capsized' and 'From A Closet In Norway (Oslo Blues)' delve into the struggles and uncertainties that come with love and relationships, addressing themes of heartbreak and reconciliation. The lyrics are reflective and heartfelt, with a poetic quality that complements the album's folk-inspired sound.

Beyond themes of love and relationships, *Rose Ave.* reflects on the human condition and the broader journey of life. Tracks like 'Break The Cycle' and 'You And Me' explore themes of hope, perseverance, and the quest for understanding.

After finishing the recordings, the duo handed the project to the record label. The name You+Me came from a card Green saw that read 'You and Me', which felt perfect for their collaboration. The album's name was inspired by the studio location.

Although Pink had become known for her specific brand of pop rock by this point in her career, when promoting *Rose Ave.*, she keenly described her musical journey from singing opera as a child to having a punk rock band, being a skater chick, to eventually signing with an R&B label. Similarly, Green shared his diverse influences, from grunge bands like Alice in Chains and Soundgarden to R&B artists like Mary J. Blige and Sade. Their eclectic backgrounds contributed to the unique sound of *Rose Ave.*

Released on 14th October 2014 through RCA and Dine Alone records, *Rose Ave.* debuted at number one on the Canadian Albums Chart, with 23,000 copies sold in its first week. In the US, the album debuted at number four on the Billboard 200, selling 50,000 copies. The album also entered the top ten charts in several other countries, including the UK, Australia, New Zealand, Germany, Switzerland, and Austria.

The Guardian said of how the two voices on the album complement each other: "The pair explore pastoral byways, and it's a partnership of equals – while Pink often dominates their harmonies due to the featheriness of Green's voice, she gives him plenty of space."

Before the album's release, three of the songs from You+Me had premiered on the duo's Vevo channel. Both musicians took the opportunity to explain their collaboration and songwriting process in two videos posted on their channel.

The first single, 'You and Me', was released on 8th September 2014, followed by 'Break The Cycle' and 'Capsized'. Pink wrote 'Break The Cycle' as a letter to her mother, who sometimes found the young Alicia Moore's rebellious youthful antics difficult to deal with.

You+Me's first performance took place on 9th October 2014, in Santa Monica, California. On 11th October 2014, Pink and Dallas Green were interviewed on National Public Radio, where they discussed their collaboration. On 13th October, the duo performed 'You and Me' on *The Ellen DeGeneres Show*, where Pink also participated in an interview. Two days later, on 15th October, videos of their first live performance were released on the You+Me official Vevo channel.

The duo continued their promotional appearances with a performance of 'You and Me' on *The Jimmy Kimmel Show* on 16th October. On 23rd October, they performed at the Los Angeles House of Blues, with the proceeds benefiting Saint John's Health Centre's cancer prevention program.

Regarding the future of You+Me, both Pink and Green embraced the uncertainty. They hadn't planned much beyond making music together, choosing to enjoy the freedom that came with it. Pink expressed an interest in playing more live shows together, whether on a larger stage or even in their living rooms for family and friends. The spontaneity and absence of strict plans had certainly added to the fun and made the collaboration enjoyable for all.

Indeed, Pink would go on to embrace further collaboration opportunities within country music. On 1st August 2016, she would collaborate with country singer Kenny Chesney on his single, 'Setting The World On Fire'. The song topped the Billboard Hot Country Songs chart and went Platinum in both the US and Canada.

Rose Ave. was a worthwhile project for Pink, allowing her to enjoy creating something different from what her fans may have been expecting. The album sold well despite how she and Green made it for pleasure and without a commercial goal in mind. It added another string to Pink's bow, showing a different side of her as an artist; the project's focus on folk and acoustic music offered a refreshing change of pace.

CHAPTER TEN
ABOUT US

In March 2014, it had been reported that Pink had signed a new multi-album record deal with RCA Records. Then, following the release and promotion of *Rose Ave.* that started in October 2014, Pink took a hiatus from her career. During this break though, she still released some music. Notably, she recorded 'Today's The Day,' which became the theme song for the thirteenth season of *The Ellen DeGeneres Show*.

In February 2016, it was announced that Pink would cover the Beatles' song 'Lucy In The Sky With Diamonds' for the Netflix original series *Beat Bugs*. That same month, it was revealed that she had recorded a cover of 'White Rabbit' – the 1967 Jefferson Airplane song written by Grace Slick – for the film *Alice Through The Looking Glass*. However, the cover was only used for the film's promotional material. She also contributed an original song, 'Just Like Fire,' to the movie's soundtrack, which went on to top the ARIA Charts in Australia.

In April 2016, Pink posted on her Instagram account that she was in the process of writing for her upcoming album, leading to speculation about a potential release later that year. However, the album's creation and release were postponed to 2017 after Pink gave birth to her second child, a son named Jameson Moon Hart on 26th December 2016. (Notably though, by July 2016, Pink had written a song called 'Recovering' for Celine Dion).

On 10th March 2017, Pink joined forces with Australian artist Sia for Stargate's debut single, 'Waterfall.' It wouldn't be until July 2017 that Pink announced she was filming a music video for an upcoming single of her own. She later shared a recording from the video set on her social media, captioning it, "Video #new

#fyeah #itsallhappening."

The development process for the album that came to be titled *Beautiful Trauma* spanned three years, the longest Pink has ever taken to work on an album. Early writing sessions proved challenging, with Pink recalling that she had spent a year writing slow and sad songs. She mentioned that during this period, she "didn't have anything to say, except for dumb sad stuff." Despite these struggles, Pink found that her career hiatus was beneficial, helping her to regain inspiration and "find [her] voice again." During this break, she focused on her family and lived a "normal life," with experiences that would influence her music.

In an interview with *Entertainment Weekly*, Pink would go on to state that *Beautiful Trauma* reflects her life at the time, with her aim being "to be as honest as [she] could." She drew inspiration for her songwriting from several personal and significant events, including a miscarriage, the 2016 US presidential election, and her father's cancer diagnosis.

Pink collaborated with a variety of producers and songwriters for *Beautiful Trauma*, bringing in familiar names like Billy Mann, Greg Kurstin, Max Martin, and Shellback, as well as new collaborators like Johnny McDaid, Julia Michaels, and Jack Antonoff. Over the course of the album's development, around fifty songs were worked on, including 'Wild Hearts Can't Be Broken.' This song had initially been written for the 2015 historical period drama film *Suffragette*, and drew inspiration from the early twentieth-century movement of the same name.

Another track, 'You Get My Love,' was written and produced by Pink and Tobias Jesso Jr. at the Earthstar Creation Centre in Venice. It was recorded in 2016 while Pink was pregnant, an experience she went on to describe as "very sober." Pink stated that 'You Get My Love' represents "the best vocal performance [she's] ever done in [her] life," attributing her vocal style to the influence of American singer Nina Simone.

In 2016, Pink co-wrote 'I Am Here' with Billy Mann and Christian Medice in Los Angeles. In the following year, she contacted Mann in July with the intention of recording the song with a local gospel choir. They travelled to Philadelphia and booked a recording session at Houser Audio with a thirty-piece choir. Mann and Bill Jolly arranged the choir's vocals, with Jolly also conducting.

'Revenge' was written by Pink, Max Martin, and Shellback. After writing rap verses, Pink thought the song would be perfect for Eminem. She sent him an email asking if he would collaborate with her again. Four days later, while Eminem was in Rio de Janeiro, he responded positively to her request; he sent her an email with his recorded verse. Pleased to work with Eminem again, Pink described him as a "lyrical genius" and "one of the best."

Beautiful Trauma is primarily a pop album that includes elements of electronic dance music and folk music. Lyrically, the album delves into emotional themes, exploring insecurities and imperfect relationships while also touching on societal and global issues. Many of the songs examine motherhood, married life, and the state of the world. There are a significant number of ballads with dramatic choruses.

Pink would go on to explain that her vocal style is different on *Beautiful Trauma* compared to her previous work, stating that her voice had become clearer due to her pregnancy.

The opening and title track is a power pop and pop rock song produced by Jack Antonoff. Its composition features "hammered" piano chords, supported by synthesisers and an orchestra. The lyrics explore a long-term troubled relationship, comparing it to drug addiction.

'Revenge', which Pink went on to describe as a "funny record," is a bad-romance duet with Eminem. The song alternates between rap and sung sections, focusing on themes of betrayal and cheating. (Pink would work with Eminem again in the future. He went on to announce on 5th December 2017 that she would be collaborating with him on 'Need Me', a track for his ninth studio album, *Revival*. It would go on to receive a Grammy nomination for Best Pop Vocal Album.)

'Whatever You Want' is a confessional pop rock song produced by Max Martin and Shellback. It was inspired by the challenges Pink faced in her relationship with her husband. Critics have noted similarities between this track and Radiohead's 'High And Dry' from 1995, pointing out the matching chord changes and the introspective nature of both songs. The comparison reveals commonalities in musical structure and emotional undertones, drawing connections between Pink's contemporary confessional style and Radiohead's mid-nineties alternative rock vibe.

The lyrics in 'Whatever You Want' delve into Pink's personal experiences with her husband, addressing the challenges and conflicts that arise in long-term relationships. They are honest and raw, capturing the complexity of love and commitment. Similarly, Radiohead's 'High And Dry' focuses on themes of isolation and emotional turmoil. Both songs explore the human condition with a level of vulnerability that resonates with listeners, further strengthening the comparison. The blend of pop rock and alternative influences is another common element between the two tracks.

'What About Us' was written by Pink, Johnny McDaid, and Steve McCutcheon, with production handled by McCutcheon. It's an electronic dance music song with a disco-style bass beat, starting as a ballad and appearing to focus on a relationship. However, the political lyrics convey a peaceful message of tolerance and unity, speaking to those who feel ignored and abandoned.

'But We Lost It' is a piano ballad, while the following track, 'Barbies', incorporates folk elements and addresses the pressure of growing up while yearning for simpler times. 'Where We Go' reflects on a damaged relationship over a guitar melody.

'For Now' is a contemporary power ballad, while 'Secrets' blends pop and funk with elements of deep house and electronic music. 'Better Life' features an R&B-infused doo-wop style and gospel undertones, with Pink comparing herself to people on social media, as evident in lyrics like "I found myself up late feeling kinda jealous/ Looking at the bullshit, other people's wellness."

'I Am Here' is an empowering track with a gospel choir, addressing Pink's journey as a person. The next track, 'Wild Hearts Can't Be Broken', written by Pink and Michael Busbee, serves as something of a feminist chant, depicting women fighting for equal rights and respect.

The final track on *Beautiful Trauma*, 'You Get My Love', is a raw and emotional piano ballad that showcases Pink's powerful vocals and expressive delivery. Her vocal runs in this track have drawn comparisons to those of legendary artists like Adele, Carole King, and Mariah Carey. These comparisons highlight Pink's ability to convey deep emotion through her voice, while also demonstrating her versatility and technical prowess. Each of the artists mentioned has a unique style and approach to singing, but Pink's performance on 'You Get My Love' – whether deliberately or coincidentally – embodies elements from each, creating a compelling and memorable ballad.

Adele is known for her powerful ballads and ability to evoke intense emotion with her voice, and Pink achieves a similar effect in this track. The vocal runs in 'You Get My Love' are rich and full of feeling, with a depth that captures the vulnerability and intimacy of the lyrics. Pink's voice soars over the piano accompaniment, creating a captivating performance that resonates with listeners.

Carole King's music often has a raw and personal quality, with a focus on storytelling and conveying genuine emotion. In 'You Get My Love', Pink embraces a similar style, using her voice to convey the heartfelt intimacy behind the song's lyrics. The stripped-down piano ballad allows Pink's vocals to take centre stage, emphasising the personal and intimate nature of the track. This approach creates a sense of connection with the listener, reminiscent of the emotional depth that Carole King is known for.

The comparison to Mariah Carey is plausibly on account of the technical prowess and vocal flexibility that Pink employs on 'You Get My Love.' Mariah Carey is famous for her vocal runs and wide range, and Pink demonstrates her own impressive vocal agility on that particular track. The dynamic vocal runs showcase Pink's ability to navigate complex melodies with precision and control. Her technical skill adds to the emotional impact of the song, allowing her to explore different vocal nuances while maintaining a strong and consistent performance.

The artwork for *Beautiful Trauma* was unveiled when the album was announced on 9th August 2017. The cover, photographed by Kurt Iswarienko, features Pink standing in front of a rundown gas station in a desert. She is dressed in a bejewelled bustier and a white gown under a large silver jacket, with reflective sunglasses and hoop earrings. The contrast between the glamorous and the gritty is evident, which seems to tie in with the meaning behind the album's title.

Pink explained that the album's title refers to the various atrocities happening around the world and her desire to focus on life's positive aspects. In an interview with *The Guardian*, she said, "I named the album *Beautiful Trauma* because life is fucking traumatic. There's natural disasters at every turn... but there's beautiful people in the world that are having a blast and being good to each other and helping others. Because I can be dark, I try to constantly remind myself that there's more good than bad."

Released on 13th October 2017, *Beautiful Trauma* debuted at the top of the US Billboard 200 chart, selling 408,000 album-equivalent units in its first week, with 384,000 of those being pure album sales. This marked Pink's second consecutive number one album on the Billboard 200. The strong sales were partly due to her tour audience, as the cost of the album was bundled into the purchase price of a tour ticket for US and Canadian shows. However, the album only counted towards sales when a ticket purchaser redeemed it. It's estimated that about 225,000 of the first-week sales came from the album-ticket bundling.

Beautiful Trauma achieved the highest first-week sales for an album by a female artist since Beyoncé's *Lemonade* (2016). It also had the highest first-week traditional album sales since Drake's *Views* (2016) and became Pink's best opening week in terms of sales. In its second week, the album dropped to number three on the Billboard 200, with sales decreasing by eighty-four percent to 64,000 units.

Beautiful Trauma sold 628,000 copies in the US throughout 2017, making it the seventh-highest-selling album of the year. In the week ending 17th May 2018, the album experienced a significant jump, climbing eighty-one places on the Billboard 200 from number eighty-three to number two, with sales of 139,000 units, including 135,000 pure album sales. This increase in sales was largely due to the album-ticket bundling that accompanied the second US leg of Pink's tour. The album would go on to be certified platinum in April 2018 by the Recording Industry Association of America (RIAA) for selling over a million equivalent units in the US.

On the Canadian Albums Chart, *Beautiful Trauma* debuted at number one, with 64,000 album-equivalent units sold, giving it the second-highest opening week in 2017 in Canada, behind Shania Twain's *Now*. It became Pink's second album to top the Canadian chart, following *The Truth About Love*. In the week ending 2nd June 2018, *Beautiful Trauma* would return to the top of the Canadian chart, selling an additional 16,000 units due to the ticket bundle campaign. It was certified double Platinum by Music Canada (MC), indicating 160,000 units sold.

Beautiful Trauma debuted at the top of the UK albums chart with first-week sales of 70,074 album-equivalent units. This marked Pink's second number one album in the UK, following *Funhouse*. By the end of 2017, *Beautiful Trauma* had sold 372,000 copies, becoming the UK's highest-selling album of the year by a non-British act and the fifth highest overall. By February 2019, the album had gone on to sell 516,087 copies in the UK and received Platinum certification from the British Phonographic Industry (BPI) for sales exceeding 300,000 units.

In Australia, *Beautiful Trauma* sold 50,000 copies within three days of its release, debuting at the top of the ARIA Albums Chart with first-week sales of 78,040 copies. This was the second-largest opening week of the year, behind Ed Sheeran's ÷ (*Divide*). Total sales in Australia exceeded 100,000 copies by the second week, keeping the album at number one. This made *Beautiful Trauma* the third album of 2017 to remain at the top for more than a week, following the *Trolls* soundtrack and ÷ (*Divide*). The album went on to spend six non-consecutive weeks at number one, the longest run by a female artist in the country since Adele's *25* in 2015. In 2017, *Beautiful Trauma* would finish as the second-highest-selling album in Australia to receive a quadruple Platinum certification from the Australian Recording Industry Association (ARIA) for sales exceeding 280,000 units.

In New Zealand, the album also debuted at the top of the Official New Zealand Music Chart, holding the position for three consecutive weeks. It received double Platinum certification from Recorded Music NZ for shipments of over 30,000 units.

Across Europe, *Beautiful Trauma* reached the top of the charts in Austria, Belgium (Flanders), the Czech Republic, and Switzerland, while also landing in the top ten in other countries. In France, the album debuted at number two on the Syndicat National de l'Édition Phonographique (SNEP) albums chart, with first-week sales of 14,853 copies, making it Pink's highest-charting album there. *Beautiful Trauma* would eventually exceed 100,000 units in sales to be certified Platinum by SNEP.

According to the International Federation of the Phonographic Industry (IFPI) – the organisation that represents the interests of the recording industry worldwide – *Beautiful Trauma* was the third and eighth best-selling album of 2017 and 2018 respectively and had sold over three-million copies worldwide by March 2019.

The album fared generally well in reviews. *USA Today* praised the "stripped-back arrangements" for emphasising Pink's abilities as a singer-songwriter and observed that the themes gravitate towards "her tumultuous relationship with Hart" and "achingly relatable anecdotes" about marriage, family, and maturing.

The Irish Times was complementary of Pink's consistent release of "relatable pop songs" throughout her career. *Entertainment Weekly* commended the album's "fresh and familiar" sound. Indeed, even Pink's manager Roger Davies referred to the album as "a continuation of the previous records."

So was it problematic that Pink's sound on *Beautiful Trauma* didn't deviate too far from her previous albums? Not necessarily. Sometimes there's a comfort in consistency that resonates with both the musician and their audience. Instead of exploring radically different musical territories, Pink leaned into what she does best: pop-rock anthems with bold lyrics and powerful vocals.

Pink has built her career on a foundation of powerful pop-rock anthems, unapologetic lyrics, and a strong vocal presence. By continuing in this vein with *Beautiful Trauma*, she affirmed her musical identity, demonstrating that her style and message remain as relevant as ever. This consistency in musical identity can be crucial in an industry where trends come and go, providing a stable foundation for continued success.

Pink's decision not to move too far from her established sound on *Beautiful Trauma* also meant that she was meeting fan expectations. Her fans had come to expect a certain level of energy, intensity, and emotional honesty from her music, and the album delivered on these fronts. By reinforcing her unique style and maintaining a strong connection with her audience, Pink ensured that *Beautiful Trauma* would be a compelling addition to her discography, continuing her legacy of bold and powerful pop-rock music.

As part of the promotional effort for *Beautiful Trauma*, on 6th September 2017, Pink held a special concert at The Theatre in the Ace Hotel in Los Angeles, where she premiered tracks from the album to an audience of specially invited fans. That same day, she appeared on *The Ellen DeGeneres Show* and performed 'What About Us.'

On 8th September 2017, Pink performed on BBC Radio One's *Live Lounge*, where she sang 'What About Us,' 'Who Knew,' 'Try,' and a cover of Sam Smith's 'Stay With Me.' On 22nd September 2017, Pink performed at the iHeartRadio Music Festival, where she delivered a medley that included 'Raise Your Glass,' 'What About Us,' 'Funhouse,' 'Just Like Fire,' and 'So What.'

With the release of *Beautiful Trauma* on 13th October 2017, Pink partnered with Apple Music to release the short documentary titled *On The Record: P!nk – Beautiful Trauma*. It featured scenes from the album's recording sessions. The following day, she appeared on *Saturday Night Live*, where she performed 'What About Us' and 'Beautiful Trauma' for the first time on television. Two days later, Pink was interviewed on *Good Morning America* and performed both of these tracks.

On 22nd October 2017, Pink took the stage at CBS Radio's We Can Survive benefit concert at the Hollywood Bowl, in support of breast cancer awareness. Her setlist included 'Barbies,' 'What About Us,' and 'Beautiful Trauma.'

On 1st November 2017, Pink appeared on *Jimmy Kimmel Live!* and sang 'What About Us.' A week later, on 8th November she performed 'Barbies' at the fifty-first Annual Country Music Association Awards, with a string quartet and two backing vocalists. *Rolling Stone* would describe this performance as "stunning and thoughtful."

On 15th November, Pink appeared on *The Late Late Show* with James Corden for the Carpool Karaoke segment, singing some of her past hits alongside 'What About Us' and 'Beautiful Trauma.'

At the 2017 American Music Awards, Pink performed 'Beautiful Trauma' while suspended by a high wire and walking on the side of the JW Marriott Hotel in Los Angeles. She collaborated with the aerial dance group Bandaloop for this highly choreographed performance, which featured backward flips and other complex acrobatic moves. The performance received positive reviews from critics, with *Billboard* naming it the best performance of the night, adding that "what makes Pink such a special performance is that no matter the setting, it's still about the vocals first."

In the UK, Pink promoted her album by performing 'What About Us' on *The Graham Norton Show* on 1st December 2017. Two days later, she performed the same song, along with 'Beautiful Trauma', on the finale of the fourteenth series of *The X Factor UK*.

For 5th December 2017, Pink travelled to France to perform a concert at the Élysée Montmartre in Paris as part of the NRJ Music Tour. She later appeared on the French television show *Quotidien* for an interview and performed 'What About Us.' On 10th December, she took to the stage again to perform 'What About Us' on *The Voice Of Germany*.

In 2018, Pink attended the sixtieth Annual Grammy Awards and performed 'Wild Hearts Can't Be Broken', accompanied on stage by an American Sign Language (ASL) interpreter. *People* called the performance "emotional," while *Billboard* opined that Pink "nailed the impossibly high notes at the song's emotional climax." Following the performance, Pink released a music video for the song. Shot in black-and-white and directed by Sasha Samsonova, it sees Pink singing while sitting alone in a barren room, wearing a simple white tank top and distressed jeans. *Entertainment Tonight* asserted that it was "one of [Pink's] most powerful music videos yet."

As well as a vibrantly busy promotional effort, the success of *Beautiful Trauma* was bolstered by the release of several singles.

'What About Us' was released as the lead single on 10th August 2017. The track received positive reviews from music critics, who praised its lyrical content, production, and Pink's vocals. Commercially, the song was a hit, reaching number one on the national charts of eight countries and landing in the top ten in twelve others.

In the US, 'What About Us' peaked at number thirteen on the Billboard Hot 100 and topped both the Adult Contemporary and Adult Pop Songs charts. It was certified Platinum by the Recording Industry Association of America (RIAA), signifying sales of one-million certified units.

The accompanying music video, directed by Georgia Hudson and choreographed by Nick Florez and RJ Durell (collectively known as the Golden Boyz), was released on 16th August 2017. The video's central theme focuses on a lost generation of abandoned and unheard people finding unity through the power of dance, which symbolises love and connection.

'Revenge' had originally been intended as the second single from *Beautiful Trauma*, but plans changed, and the title track was released instead. 'Beautiful Trauma' was made available as a promotional single on 28th September 2017 and officially released to US contemporary hit radio stations on 21st November. Commercially, the song performed moderately on various charts, reaching top forty positions in over ten countries, including the UK, Australia, and Belgium.

To support the release, a music video for 'Beautiful Trauma' was produced, directed by the Golden Boyz. The video depicts a married couple – Pink as a 1950s housewife and her husband, played by Channing Tatum – engaging in their daily routines and dancing on vibrant, colourful sets. As the video progresses, the couple explore an "experimental phase" involving cross-dressing and S&M themes.

One week before the release of *Beautiful Trauma*, 'Whatever You Want' was issued as a promotional single on 5th October 2017. A music video for the song was released on 1st March 2018, featuring scenes of Pink preparing for her Beautiful Trauma World Tour. The video also included footage from her performance at Super Bowl LII (at which she performed brilliantly, despite suffering from a bout of flu at the time), her appearance at the 2017 MTV Video Music Awards, and clips from the documentary *On The Record: P!nk – Beautiful Trauma*. The song was later sent to US adult contemporary radio stations on 4th June 2018 as the album's third single. It reached number eleven on the US Adult top forty chart and number twenty-two on the Adult Contemporary chart.

'Secrets' was released as the fourth and final single from *Beautiful Trauma* in Europe, accompanied by a four-track remix EP. The music video for the song was co-directed by Pink and Larn Poland, and was filmed in Northbridge, Western Australia. Released on 24th July 2018, it features Pink and her dancers performing in a graffiti-covered warehouse. 'Secrets' became a hit on the US Dance Club Songs chart, reaching the number one spot. It was the third song from *Beautiful Trauma* to top this chart, following 'What About Us' and the album's title track.

It was on 5th October 2017 that Pink announced she would embark on her seventh concert tour, the Beautiful Trauma World Tour. Initially, the tour included seventeen shows in Oceania, but due to high demand, additional dates were added.

A month after having collaborated with Elton John and Logic on a rendition of 'Bennie And The Jets' for Elton John's album, *Revamp & Restoration*, on 3rd May 2018, Pink announced a second North American leg for the tour. Set to start in 2019, it would include rescheduled shows for Detroit and Montreal. In October of that year, the tour was extended further into 2019 with a European leg. The 2019 shows would serve to promote Pink's eighth studio album, *Hurts 2 B Human*.

In reference to the first show of the tour which took place in Phoenix, US, *The Arizona Republic* opined that "the whole thing was brilliantly staged, with bright colours, interpretive dancing and plenty of high-flying spectacle. If for some reason, you believe you've seen another artist put more time and effort into doing acrobatics high above the crowd, you may just be thinking of Cirque du Soleil." (The comparison is justified; between the ages of four and twelve, Pink had trained as a competitive gymnast.)

Of the performance in Lincoln, US, the *Omaha World-Herald* noted that Pink has "set the bar very, very high" and that "her contemporaries should buy a ticket, sit in the back and take notes. That's how it should be done." Lincoln's *Journal Star* said, "When she wasn't flying around, Pink was in constant motion on the stage, joining her ten dancers in tightly choreographed routines, slapping hands with audience members and basking in the spotlights."

Of the first show of the tour in Oceania, *The West Australian* called the tour Pink's "best yet" due to it having "the perfect mix of choreography, visuals, aerial acrobatics, pyrotechnics, novelty, sass and yes, that soaring voice that rises above any notion that she is just a robot on autopilot."

In the UK, *The Guardian* rated the Cardiff show five out of five stars, stating, "Pink condenses a tour's worth of energy, showmanship and stage production into one show, flexing her athleticism while singing live, on-key and with sublime verve."

It's nothing short of phenomenal that Pink received such unanimously good reviews for her performances on her Beautiful Trauma World Tour. The consistent praise from critics and fans alike underscored Pink's unique talent as a live performer and her dedication to creating unforgettable concert experiences. These unanimously positive reviews served as testament to Pink's status as one of the most dynamic and captivating performers in the music industry.

A masterclass in theatricality and raw energy, Pink's performances featured high-flying acrobatics, intricate stage setups, and elaborate choreography – all elements that contributed to the tour's overwhelmingly positive reception.

With a mixture of high-energy anthems, emotional ballads, and fan favourites, the setlist was diverse and dynamic, allowing Pink to showcase her versatility as an artist. The seamless transitions between different musical styles and the flawless execution of each song offered something for everyone.

In total, the Beautiful Trauma World Tour consisted of 159 shows: eighty-nine in North America, forty-two in Oceania, twenty-seven in Europe, and one in South America. It achieved significant commercial success, ranking as the eleventh-highest-grossing tour of all time, and the second-highest-grossing tour of all time by a female solo artist, generating $397,300,000 from over three-million tickets sold.

The last tour date of 2018 was 19th September at Qudos Bank Arena, Sydney, Australia. Following this, Pink's fans still had another treat in store: On 23rd October, as part of the album *The Greatest Showman – Reimagined*, Pink's version of 'A Million Dreams' was released. The album reinterpreted the original soundtrack with contributions from artists including Kelly Clarkson, Kesha, Jess Glynne, and Missy Elliott. Pink's daughter, Willow Sage Hart, also contributed by performing 'A Million Dreams (Reprise).'

The *Beautiful Trauma* period of Pink's career demonstrated once again that she was an artist at the top of her game. Despite the five-year gap between *The Truth About Love* and *Beautiful Trauma*, Pink's 2017 album release was marked by overwhelming success, both commercially and critically. If anything, it could be the case that the gap had served to create a sense of anticipation and excitement for fans awaiting a new studio album.

Through chart-topping singles, innovative production, and deeply personal lyrics, *Beautiful Trauma* showed that Pink hadn't lost her touch but had instead come back with a whole new set of songs that would hit the mark, proving her enduring appeal and versatility as an artist. Also, as a mother to two children by that point in her career, Pink's willingness to share her personal experiences and vulnerabilities added depth to the album, reinforcing her reputation as an artist who isn't afraid to be genuine. This authenticity plausibly played a significant role in the album's success, with fans appreciating the realness and relatability that Pink once again had brought to her music.

CHAPTER ELEVEN
HUSTLE

Creating an album while committed to tour responsibilities is a daunting challenge for any artist. The demands of touring – constant travel, intense performances, and promotional obligations – can leave little room for the creative process required to produce a new album.

Yet some artists manage to navigate these difficulties, balancing the demands of life on the road with the need for studio time, inspiration, and personal reflection. The challenge lies in finding the right equilibrium between these conflicting commitments, ensuring that neither the tour nor the album suffers from the strain. With her eighth studio album, *Hurts 2B Human*, Pink certainly had her work cut out, but still, she persevered.

The recording sessions for *Hurts 2B Human* happened while Pink was on the Beautiful Trauma World Tour, resulting in the composition of up to twenty songs that were considered for inclusion. Pink would go on to explain that the creative process for making *Hurts 2B Human* was different from her previous projects. Previously, she had typically been in the habit of doing no writing whilst on tour. During the Beautiful Trauma World Tour, however, she kept creating new music. Initially, the plan had been to record a standalone EP, but as the sessions continued, it turned into a full album. Pink said it "came together without me knowing that I was making an album."

Recording sessions were held at several studios, including The Village Studios, MXM Studios, and Echo Studio in Los Angeles, as well as Earthstar Creation Centre in Venice, Grand Central South in Brentwood, Wolf Cousins Studios in Stockholm, and Roundhead Studios in Auckland. Pink would describe the development process as something that started as a small pebble rolling downhill that eventually became a large boulder.

Pink would describe *Hurts 2B Human* as a shift from the "angsty and marital" themes of her previous records, likening the songs to group therapy. The inspiration for the album came from the melancholy and pressures of contemporary society, with pain being a central motivator and topic of discussion. Pink would also credit motherhood for positively influencing her music and her life, making her more open, confident, and thoughtful.

Hurts 2B Human features collaborations with several notable musicians. Pink invited Los Angeles-based singer, songwriter and musician Wrabel to her home studio, where they wrote '90 Days' with Steve Robson. Wrabel went on to tell *Get Out!* magazine that the song explores themes ranging from falling out of love to becoming sober, which he said made the song particularly special for him. '90 Days' is a minimalist electronica ballad with a piano and vocoder-enhanced harmonies.

Admiring his voice, Pink approached Texan singer and songwriter Khalid for the title track, 'Hurts 2B Human.' It has an EDM beat, plucky electric guitar chords, and synths. The lyrics reflect the everyday struggles people face, whilst celebrating the unifying power of overcoming those struggles together.

Pink would go on to explain that the song's lyrics centre on the human experience and how a good support network can help a person to overcome difficult times.

'Can We Pretend' features the electronic group Cash Cash. Pink shared that she had a fun experience creating the song. It's an electronic dance music and dance-pop track. It explores the idea of using nostalgia to escape the harshness of reality.

For 'Love Me Anyway', Pink was inspired by Lee Ann Womack's 'I Hope You Dance.' She reached out to Chris Stapleton for a collaboration, and following his positive response, travelled to Nashville to co-write the country ballad with Allen Shamblin and Tom Douglas. The lyrics refer to commitment in a relationship and the challenges that can occur. Whilst Stapleton's voice fades into the background to an extent, it very much works as a duet. On having the opportunity to work with Stapleton, Pink would go on to describe it as "one of the greatest honours of my life."

Hurts 2B Human is a pop album that blends elements of dance and country music, featuring mostly radio-friendly power ballads. The opening track, 'Hustle', is an upbeat pop song with country influences. The lyrics explore a relationship gone wrong, with Pink warning her partner that he can't take advantage of her again.

'(Hey Why) Miss You Sometime' is a dance-pop song where Pink expresses that she misses someone who hurt her in the past. The track features heavily auto-tuned vocals.

'Walk Me Home' is a pop song with country elements and digitised vocal production.

'My Attic' is an introspective ballad with raspy vocals and poetic lyrics about storing memories and secrets.

'Courage' is an acoustic power ballad that gradually builds, featuring anxious-sounding vocals.

'Happy' is a vulnerable song where Pink shares her insecurities from growing up and the fear of opening up. She sings, "Since I was seventeen, I've always hated my body, and it feels like my body's hated me." Pink would go on to reveal that this line was influenced by a miscarriage she experienced at that age, which led to feelings of self-rejection and a sense that her body wasn't functioning as it should.

'We Could Have It All' is a pop rock song with a heavy groove. The song seems to capture the feeling of defeat that can occur after having ruined something good and not knowing how to fix it.

'Circle Game', the penultimate track, reflects on motherhood, mortality, and growing up to become a parental figure. This piano-driven ballad is something of a personal track. It explores Pink's relationship with her daughter and the childhood vulnerabilities that she herself has carried into adulthood. Pink would go on to reveal that the song was inspired by her dad, who was her first hero and taught her to fight for what she believes in.

Hurts 2B Human concludes with 'The Last Song Of Your Life', an acoustic folk ballad with melancholic undertones. The song is a heartfelt plea for honesty and authenticity, with a strong sense of finality.

Hurts 2B Human was released on 26th April 2019, just eighteen months after *Beautiful Trauma* – the shortest gap between studio albums in Pink's career. Multiple singles were released to promote the album.

Prior to the release of the album's singles, on 5th February 2019, Pink received a star on the Hollywood Walk of Fame. Of course, to be awarded a star there goes beyond the fact that a person is merely famous; it marks a celebration of a career built on talent and hard work. To receive a star on the Walk of Fame is a prestigious honour, symbolising an artist's lasting impact on the entertainment industry.

The lead single, 'Walk Me Home' was released on 20th February 2019. Pink performed it as part of a medley at the 2019 Brit Awards on the same day. Critics praised the single for its anthemic approach and production. The song achieved commercial success, reaching the top ten in several countries including the UK, Ireland, Finland, and Switzerland. In the US, it peaked within the top fifty on the Billboard Hot 100 chart, topped the Dance Club Songs chart, and reached number one on both the Adult Contemporary and Adult Pop Songs charts. The single also received a nomination for Best Song at the 2020 Global Awards. The music video, directed by Michael Gracey, was released a month after the single's debut. It features Pink dancing with multiple shadows in an empty city.

'Hustle' was released on 28th March, coinciding with the album's pre-order date. Following this, 'Can We Pretend' debuted on 11th April. It was later released as the second official single in Australia in May, and then to adult contemporary radio stations in the US on 22nd July 2019. It reached number one on the Billboard Dance Club Songs chart.

It was on 22nd April that the album's title track was unveiled as the third promotional single. On the same day, Pink performed 'Walk Me Home' on *The Ellen DeGeneres Show*. Continuing the promotional trail, Pink appeared on *Jimmy Kimmel Live!* on 1st May, where she performed 'Hustle.'

The music video for '90 Days', showcasing the challenges of being a touring musician with a family, premiered on 18th June. Ten days later, the animated music video for 'Can We Pretend' was released, depicting Pink embarking on a space exploration adventure.

'Hurts 2B Human' was released as the album's third single on 30th August in selected territories. 'Love Me Anyway' was initially introduced to country radio on 17th September, and later, on 18th November, to adult contemporary radio in the US as the final single from *Hurts 2B Human*.

Accompanying the release of 'Hurts 2B Human', a music video directed by Alissa Torvinen premiered on 18th November. Set in a New York City apartment, it portrays individuals coping with the daily stresses of life.

Pink performed 'Love Me Anyway' with Chris Stapleton at the fifty-third Annual Country Music Association Awards on 13th November.

Hurts 2B Human made a strong debut at number one on the US Billboard 200 chart, selling 115,000 album-equivalent units in the week ending 2nd May. This marked Pink's third album to reach the top spot on the chart, following *The Truth About Love* and *Beautiful Trauma*. It was also the second-best-selling album of the week in pure album sales, with 95,000 copies. By June 2019, the album had sold 158,000 pure album copies in the US. In Canada, *Hurts 2B Human* also debuted at number one, with first-week sales of 13,000 units.

Hurts 2B Human debuted at the top of the UK Albums Chart, selling 48,861 copies in its first week, with 4,359 coming from stream-equivalent units. This first-week performance outsold its closest competitor – *The Balance* by Catfish and the Bottlemen – by 22,000 units, marking Pink's third album to reach number one in the UK. The following week, the album stayed at the top, with 16,713 equivalent units sold, making it Pink's first album to spend more than a week at number one in the UK.

The album held the number one position for a third consecutive week, selling 11,582 equivalent units. Due to its successful sales, *Hurts 2B Human* received a Silver certification from the British Phonographic Industry (BPI) for surpassing 60,000 units sold. Across Europe, the album also reached number one in Belgium, Ireland, the Netherlands, Scotland, and Switzerland, while charting within the top ten in several other countries.

In Australia, *Hurts 2B Human* debuted at the top of the ARIA

Albums Chart, becoming Pink's sixth album to reach number one there. This achievement marked her forty-first week at the top of the chart, breaking her tie with Adele and placing her at number five on the list of artists with the most accumulated weeks at number one.

Pink also became the female artist with the most cumulative weeks at the top and ranked second on the list of female artists with the most chart-topping albums, with only Madonna ahead of her. *Hurts 2B Human* stayed at number one for a total of three weeks and earned a Platinum certification from the Australian Recording Industry Association (ARIA), signifying 70,000 units shipped.

In New Zealand, *Hurts 2B Human* also debuted at number one on the Official New Zealand Music Chart, becoming Pink's third chart-topping album. It achieved a Gold certification from Recorded Music NZ for shipments exceeding 7,500 units.

Hurts 2B Human was met with generally positive reviews. *Entertainment Weekly* commented that the optimistic nature of the album makes it enjoyable and relatable, and found country pop influences that show "how [Pink's] true-to-life lyrics and soulful bellow can play in Nashville's finest honky-tonks."

The *Los Angeles Times* considered that *Hurts 2B Human* comes across as "strikingly aligned," pointing out how the messages about "overcoming obstacles and learning to trust in [your own] abilities" contrast with the music of younger artists that tend to approach topics such as depression and drug consumption.

Stereogum opined that *Hurts 2B Human* showcases an artist "who's found her comfort zone and has successfully grown her music up along with her."

Indeed, it's interesting that Pink embraced a more country-style sound for some of the songs on *Hurts 2B Human*. Having predominantly built her early career on edgy pop-rock and anthemic ballads, Pink's foray into country elements marked a shift in her musical exploration. Not only did it demonstrate her versatility as an artist, but also served to tap into a broader audience. The addition of country-style sounds and themes to her album added depth and variety, providing listeners with a fresh perspective on Pink's ever-evolving artistry.

The embrace of a more country-style sound on *Hurts 2B Human* could also be seen as a reflection of Pink's personal growth. Country music often emphasises themes of family, relationships, and life's simple pleasures, aligning with Pink's own journey as a mother and her exploration of deep emotional landscapes.

As ever, Pink's candour was evident in her approach to interviews. When promoting *Hurts 2B Human*, she told *USA Today*, "I believe in self-confrontation and just getting things out. What I love about therapy is that they'll tell you what your blind spots are. Although that's uncomfortable and painful, it gives you something to work with."

Such approach to interviews is plausibly a reflection of what Pink's broader philosophy may be – she doesn't shy away from difficult truths, whether in her music or in her personal life. This vulnerability is a key reason as to why her fans find her so relatable, and why her music resonates with so many. Her comment about the value of therapy and self-confrontation underscores her commitment to authenticity and self-reflection.

CHAPTER TWELVE
DANCE AGAIN

Following the release of *Hurts 2B Human* in 2019, Pink embarked on some collaborations. First, she worked with Keith Urban on the song 'One Too Many'. Featured on Urban's eleventh studio album, *The Speed Of Now Part 1* (2020), 'One Too Many' was written by Peter Wallevik and Daniel Davidsen (known as PhD), Cleo Tighe, James Norton (also known as Boy Matthews), and Mich Hansen (also known as Cutfather).

The concept of the song is centred on a couple trying to reconnect with one another after one of them regains consciousness following a night of drinking, with the other one trying to avoid yet another argument. Delighted at having had the opportunity to work with Pink, when promoting the single, Urban said, "I've always loved Pink's voice, but her artistry and her multi-faceted ability to create, and her God-given talent, truly makes her one of the greatest voices of our time."

Directed by Dano Cerny and released on 18th September, the music video for 'One Too Many' opens with scenes of objects floating on water, including a guitar, a telephone, and sheet music. The visuals then focus on Keith Urban, who is adrift on a floating sofa in the sea, using it as a makeshift life raft. Meanwhile, Pink is shown sitting alone on the shore, gazing out at the water. As the song progresses into the chorus, Urban and Pink harmonise, singing towards each other despite being in different locations.

Having premiered at the fifty-fifth Academy of Country Music Awards on 16th September 2020, the same day it was released as the third single from Urban's album, 'One Too Many' would go on to be played on country and pop radio stations in various regions.

It earned a nomination for Song of the Year at the 2021 ARIA Music Awards, and at the 2022 Queensland Music Awards, it won the award for Highest Selling Single of the Year.

Pink's collaboration with Keith Urban once again showcased her ability to cross genres and work with artists from different backgrounds. The song garnered attention for its catchy melody and heartfelt lyrics, but more than that, perhaps, the collaboration was both impressive and endearing in being demonstrative of Pink's willingness to explore new musical territories and build connections with more artists outside of her usual genre.

On 12th February 2021, a particularly special collaboration was released: 'Cover Me In Sunshine.' A duet featuring Pink and her daughter Willow Sage Hart, it was written by Amy Allen and Mozella with production by A Strut (Ludwig Söderberg). The song has an upbeat, mid-tempo pop sound featuring positive lyrics accompanied by acoustic guitars. Pink sings the first verse and chorus, with backing vocals contributed by her daughter. The outro is sung solely by Willow.

On 8th February 2021, Pink had shared an acappella teaser of the 'Cover Me In Sunshine' chorus, featuring her daughter singing, on her TikTok account. Two days later, Pink announced that the complete version of the song would be released on 12th February. She also shared a video highlighting the collaboration with her daughter.

"I love singing with my daughter and my son," she said. "We have this song called 'Cover Me In Sunshine' that we recorded at home because it made us feel happy and so we're going to put it out for no other reason than that we hope that the song makes you feel happy. We thought we'd put it out around Valentine's Day as a big ol' hug and a kiss from us to all y'all."

Released the same day as the single, the music video for 'Cover Me In Sunshine' is reminiscent of a traditional family home video. Recorded on Pink's family ranch and winery near Santa Barbara, California, it features the singer and her daughter having fun in nature, riding horses, collecting chicken eggs and being in a boat. (Pink had purchased the eighteen-acre organic vineyard in 2013.)

Although the song didn't place in the US on the main singles chart, it peaked at number four in the Bubbling Under Hot 100 chart with two-million streams and 11,000 downloads. It also achieved success overseas, topping the charts in Belgium, Romania and Slovakia. It hit the top ten in Australia, Austria, the Czech Republic, Germany, Latvia, the Netherlands, Norway, Slovenia, and Switzerland. In Australia, it was certified Gold by the Australian Recording Industry Association for shipping 35,000 copies.

The overall praise from US-based critics was generally positive. *Entertainment Tonight* called the duo "the cutest twosome around" and described Willow Sage Hart's voice as "impressive." *Billboard* called the song "inspirational" and "dreamy," while describing its chorus as "bright and poppy."

An emotionally driven piano-centred ballad written by Pink and Rag'n'Bone Man, 'Anywhere Away From Here' was released as a digital download and for streaming on 9th April 2021 as the second single from Rag'n'Bone Man's second studio album, *Life By Misadventure*. The single got to number nine in the UK, where it would go on to be certified Platinum.

Pink had met Rag'n'Bone Man in Europe in 2017, and had already heard his 2016 single, 'Human'. "By then I had already fallen in love with his voice," she recalled. "When we met in person I quickly learned he has a beautiful soul too. Since then, I knew I wanted to work with him one day. 'Anywhere Away From Here' couldn't be a better song for us to sing together. I'm so honoured to be a part of this collaboration."

Rag'n'Bone Man would go on to say of 'Anywhere Away From Here', "This song is an honest reflection of wanting to disappear from uncomfortable situations – about the vulnerabilities that we all face. It's an honour to have Pink on this record and I'm so glad she is able to be a part of it."

Indeed, 'Anywhere Away From Here' is a powerful duet that succeeded to blend Pink's dynamic vocal style with Rag'n'Bone Man's soulful depth, creating a captivating and emotionally charged performance.

What's most impressive about Pink's collaborations between 2020 and 2021 is the range of artists she worked with and the genuine connections she formed. Whether singing with her daughter, Rag'n'Bone Man, or Keith Urban, Pink brought authenticity and a sense of shared purpose to each collaboration.

These partnerships highlighted her versatility as an artist, proving that she could adapt to different styles while maintaining her distinctive voice. The collaborations also reinforced Pink's reputation as a musician who values other artists and is open to exploring new creative opportunities.

On 21st May 2021, Pink released a documentary titled *All I Know So Far*, which chronicled her record-breaking Beautiful Trauma World Tour. To promote the documentary, she released 'All I Know So Far' as a single, alongside a live album. 'All I Know So Far' is based on Pink's life and career and was written as an advice-filled love letter to her daughter. It approaches themes of perseverance and strength in the face of adversity. During the promotional period for these releases, Pink was asked about her upcoming studio album's direction. She indicated that it was still in its early stages but emphasised that it would be "very honest."

In February 2022, Pink teamed up with Calm, an app focused on mindfulness, to narrate three bedtime stories. It wouldn't be until 14th July 2022 that she surprised her fans by releasing her first single since 2021, 'Irrelevant'. This protest song, written by Pink and the track's producer Ian Fitchuk, was a response to her anger over the US Supreme Court's decision to overrule Roe v. Wade.

Roe v. Wade was a landmark US Supreme Court case decided in 1973, which had effectively legalised abortion across the US. The case was named after 'Jane Roe', a pseudonym for Norma McCorvey, who challenged the abortion laws in Texas, and Henry Wade, the district attorney of Dallas County who defended the state's anti-abortion laws. The court's decision, delivered by Justice Harry Blackmun, had ruled that a woman's right to choose to have an abortion falls within the right to privacy protected by the Fourteenth Amendment to the US Constitution. The ruling established a framework that divided pregnancy into trimesters:

During the first trimester, the decision to have an abortion was left entirely to the woman and her doctor. During the second trimester, the state could regulate abortion but only to protect the mother's health. During the third trimester, the state could ban abortion except when the mother's life or health was at risk.

Roe v. Wade was highly controversial from its inception and

became a central point in the ongoing debate over abortion rights in the US. It went on to shape decades of legal and political battles around reproductive rights, influencing state and federal legislation, and becoming a significant topic in political campaigns.

In June 2022, the Supreme Court's decision in Dobbs v. Jackson Women's Health Organisation overturned Roe v. Wade, ruling that there is no constitutional right to abortion, effectively returning the power to regulate or ban abortion to individual states. This decision has had significant legal and social ramifications, leading to a new era of activism and legal battles over abortion rights in the US.

The Supreme Court's reversal of Roe v. Wade sparked widespread outrage and protests across the US, with many perceiving it as a significant setback for women's rights and reproductive freedom. Pink's 'Irrelevant' taps into this political climate, using her music to voice dissent and rally against injustice. The song's lyrics are defiant and assertive, emphasising the importance of speaking out and challenging oppressive systems.

'Irrelevant' serves as a call to action and a message of empowerment for those who feel their voices have been marginalised or dismissed. The song's chorus, with its powerful declaration that "girls just wanna have rights," aligns with the sentiments of many who believe in bodily autonomy and reproductive choice. The anthem-like quality of the song encourages listeners to stand up for their beliefs and fight against policies that threaten their freedoms.

The music video for 'Irrelevant' was directed by Pink and Brad Comfort and premiered on Pink's official YouTube channel on 18th July 2022. It features a blend of protest footage and studio clips recorded by Pink. It incorporates scenes from various civil rights protests, including marches supporting the Me Too movement, LGBT rights, Black Lives Matter, and anti-gun violence demonstrations. The visuals also showcase notable activists like Tarana Burke and Muhammad Ali, along with politicians such as Donald Trump and Rudy Giuliani. *Billboard* described the video as "chilling," asserting that it illustrates the continuity between past and present struggles for justice.

In the context of the Roe v. Wade reversal, 'Irrelevant' is an anthem for resistance, urging people to persist in their advocacy for women's rights. By releasing 'Irrelevant' during this turbulent time, Pink contributed to the cultural conversation surrounding Dobbs' decision and its impact on women's autonomy.

From May to October 2022, Pink headlined several major music festivals, including Bottlerock Napa Valley, Ohana Festival, and Austin City Limits. She also performed at the Yaamava Theatre in Southern California, the second Taylor Hawkins Tribute Concert in Los Angeles, and the Foo Fighters' Hanukkah Sessions.

Pink's ninth studio album, *Trustfall*, was written during the pandemic. It was a particularly difficult period for Pink; in 2020, her son Jameson had a severe battle with COVID-19 at the age of three, and in 2021, she lost her father to cancer.

Despite the sombre events surrounding the album's conception, Pink found reasons to stay positive. Produced with a diverse array of collaborators, *Trustfall* takes on personal trauma with an upbeat energy. Songs like 'Runaway', 'Last Call', and the title track feature up-tempo beats that underscore the theme of finding strength amid adversity.

The creation of *Trustfall* took three years, with 'Lost Cause' and 'Never Gonna Not Dance Again' being among the first songs completed. Pink would explain that 'Never Gonna Not Dance Again' was her reaction to the stress and pressure of adrenal fatigue and cortisol. The song was her way of saying that sometimes you have to let go and find joy, allowing stress to roll off your shoulders. "My album is a piece of me," she told *Good Morning America*. "I think that I am an example of how you can live authentically and fearlessly, in ways."

Trustfall is mainly a dance-pop album that integrates a mix of sub-genres, including pop rock, Americana, country music, and folk. Several tracks feature military-style drums, solo piano, and guitar stomps. The lyrics focus on themes like self-motivation, self-acceptance, afterlife, loss, and love.

A number of artists active in a broad range of genres collaborated with Pink on the making of *Trustfall*. Delighted to have worked with them, Pink would go on to post on her Twitter account, "I am so in love with this new album and CANNOT WAIT for you to hear every single song! I'm also honoured that my friends @FirstAidKitBand, @thelumineers and @ChrisStapleton came to play with me on this record."

First Aid Kit features on 'Kids In Love.' The Lumineers feature on 'Long Way To Go.' Chris Stapleton features on 'Just Say I'm Sorry,' marking Pink's second collaboration with the country singer.

In an interview with *Billboard*, Pink would admit that she knew some of the album could perhaps be considered "corny." For instance, 'Never Gonna Not Dance Again,' produced by Max Martin and Shellback, is a lively, upbeat groove that finds Pink embracing movement over worry. The song's lyrics and joyous chorus stands out as refreshingly carefree in a pop landscape often marked by irony and detachment.

Pink would acknowledge the dance-pop sound that 'Never Gonna Not Dance Again' embraces could possibly be seen as being overly similar to her previous work. "I was like, 'Well, it's kind of my formula, isn't it? That sounds like a Pink song,'" she told *Billboard*, adding, "I don't care if it's cheesy!"

Of course, embracing a bit of cheesiness wasn't done at the expense of creating an album abundant in artistic merit. Pink considered the sequencing of her album crucial, especially for listeners who might wish to experience it from start to finish. Likening life to an emotional roller coaster, with its ups and downs, she wanted the album to reflect that journey. "Life is messy and beautiful and messy again," she went on to say, keen to emphasise that the structure of the album should represent this reality.

Indeed, a fan of music across a range of genres, and unreserved in her efforts to do justice to songs by other artists, it was on 27th September 2022 that Pink attended the Taylor Hawkins Tribute Concert in Los Angeles, where she performed 'Barracuda' by Heart, 'Somebody To Love' by Queen, and 'The Pretender' by Foo Fighters.

On 18th November 2022, Pink announced *Trustfall* on *Good Morning America* and revealed its release date through her social media accounts. She had also announced on 6th October 2022 that she would embark on a UK and European tour as part of her Pink Summer Carnival Tour in 2023, with information on North American dates to come in November.

On 17th October 2022, Pink gave a preview of the album's lead single, 'Never Gonna Not Dance Again' by releasing a snippet on social media. The song became available to stream on Apple Music and Spotify on 4th November 2022. The following day, Pink had the honour of inducting Dolly Parton into the Rock and Roll Hall of Fame.

Wearing roller skates, Pink performed 'Never Gonna Not Dance Again' live for the first time at the American Music Awards on 20th November 2022. That same night, she paid tribute to Olivia Newton-John with a performance of 'Hopelessly Devoted To You'. (Olivia Newton-John had lost her battle with cancer on 8th August that year.)

Released on YouTube the same day as the single, the music video for 'Never Gonna Not Dance Again', just as upbeat as the song, features Pink roller skating through a grocery store while dressed in a colourful outfit. She continues skating into a parking lot, and by the end of the video, the grocery store has transformed into a nightclub.

On 18th January 2023, Pink revealed on social media that 'Trustfall' would be the second single from her new album and shared a snippet of the song. Directed by Georgia Hudson, the music video for the track was released the same day as the song – 27th January 2023. It features Pink alongside a young woman at a house party, who is building the courage to approach a man she's interested in. In other scenes, Pink is shown dancing on a dark street and standing on top of a hotel, with choreography by Ryan Heffington.

On 6th February 2023, Pink appeared on *The Kelly Clarkson Show* to promote the album. A week later, on 14th February, she released the third single, 'When I Get There', written by Amy Wadge and David Hodges as a tribute to Pink's late father, Jim Moore. 'Runaway' was later sent to radio stations in Australia and Germany on 7th July 2023.

On 13th October 2023, Pink announced that she would be releasing a deluxe edition of *Trustfall*. This new edition, set for release on 1st December 2023, would include her single from the past year, 'Irrelevant', along with two new songs and six live recordings from her Summer Carnival Tour. The deluxe edition would be available for digital download, as well as in LP and CD formats. Additionally, Pink announced that she would be embarking on the Trustfall Tour, a series of performances in the US between October and November 2023, as a break from the Summer Carnival Tour. The Summer Carnival Tour continued in Australia in 2024.

Released on 17th February 2023, *Trustfall* debuted at number one on the UK Albums Chart. Over sixty-five percent of its total sales were physical copies, marking it as Pink's fourth album to reach this position and her third consecutive number one album, following *Beautiful Trauma* and *Hurts 2B Human*.

Trustfall also secured the number two spot on the Official Vinyl Albums Chart. The album debuted at number one on the Australian Albums Chart, making it Pink's seventh album to reach this pinnacle there. In the US, *Trustfall* debuted at number two on the Billboard 200, achieving sales of 74,500 album-equivalent units, with 59,000 of those being pure album sales. This marked the first time since *Funhouse* that a Pink album didn't debut at number one.

Trustfall was met with a generally positive response from critics. *Rolling Stone* considered that lyrically, the songs "don't shy away from irascibility or eye-rolling" but "feel like they're coming from a genuine place" and that "Pink's appeal comes from her ability to turn the everyday into the stereo-ready."

Consequence considered that Pink was "still wearing her emotions on her sleeve, keen to embrace a deep sense of vulnerability as she processes some extremely difficult events."

CHAPTER THIRTEEN
A WOMAN OF INTEGRITY

During an interview to promote her latest album, an interviewer tactlessly asked Pink for her opinion on Madonna's current look. Of course, in recent years, Madonna has had an extent of cosmetic surgery that has changed her looks dramatically. Evidently infuriated with the interviewer's attempt at trying to trap her into saying something potentially uncomfortable and controversial about Madonna's appearance, Pink gave a no-nonsense answer:

"We shouldn't be talking about Madonna's face. We should be talking about all the badass shit that woman did for the rest of us to come along after her. But we're still pitted against each other. Everybody still wants a feud. I just worked for three years on my heart and soul of a project. I'm so proud of my album. My father died and I was able to put a song together about it, and you're asking me what I think about Madonna's face?! That is not progress."

Pink's refusal to participate in such a potentially derogatory discussion demonstrates her leadership and sets a positive example for others in the industry. She has consistently focused on her own career and artistic expression without resorting to negativity or drama to gain attention. This level of professionalism and maturity is potentially inspirational for other artists, encouraging them to take a similar approach, and fostering an environment where creativity and collaboration are valued over sensationalism and conflict. Pink sets an example, illustrating that success can be achieved through hard work and dedication, rather than by tearing others down.

Pink's stance against negative talk about other female artists contributes to a more positive industry culture. By choosing to celebrate the achievements of her peers instead of criticising them, Pink helps shift the narrative away from divisiveness and towards mutual respect. This shift is essential in an industry where women often face scrutiny and pressure to conform to certain expectations. Pink's encouragement of a positive industry culture makes it easier for women to support one another, ultimately benefiting the industry as a whole, and indeed, the impressionable public.

Although throughout her career, Pink has often spoken of her admiration for Madonna, it's clear that even if the interviewer had asked for her opinion on a different artist, Pink probably wouldn't have been willing to entertain his question.

And of course, Pink's admiration for Madonna is endearing, particularly in how it played a significant role in her early career. In a 2000 interview with MTV, Pink recalled, "I've always been the type of person that followed Madonna like a lost puppy… Madonna has always been an inspiration for me… I was a fan right from the first time I heard 'Holiday.'" The young Pink even won her first talent show by singing Madonna's 'Oh Father.'

Also an admirer of the sixties icon Janis Joplin, Pink told the *Los Angeles Times* in 2003, "She was so inspiring by singing blues music when it wasn't culturally acceptable for white women, and she wore her heart on her sleeve. She was so witty and charming and intelligent, but she also battled an ugly-duckling syndrome. I would love to play her in a movie." During a tribute performance on her Try This Tour, Pink referred to Joplin as "a woman who inspired me when everyone else ... didn't!"

Evidently someone of integrity, Pink has embraced many opportunities to use her fame and fortune to help others and speak out on several societal issues. She has been actively involved with numerous charities and campaigns, including Human Rights Campaign, ONE Campaign, The Prince's Trust, New York Restoration Project, Run for the Cure Foundation, Save the Children, Take Back the Night, UNICEF, World Animal Protection, One Billion Rising, Youth Off The Streets, Black Lives Matter, and Good Ride.

On 16th February 2009, Pink announced a donation of

$250,000 to the Red Cross Bushfire Appeal to support victims of the bushfires that had devastated the Australian state of Victoria earlier that month. Pink explained that she wanted to make "a tangible expression of support." She also contributed funds to Autism Speaks.

In December 2015, Pink was appointed as a UNICEF Ambassador and named the agency's Kid Power National Spokesperson. Her role aimed to raise awareness about UNICEF's vital health and nutrition programs worldwide. She travelled to Haiti with UNICEF to see firsthand how therapeutic food helps malnourished children.

In 2017, Pink and her husband joined a fundraising bike ride that raised two-million dollars for the Share Our Strength's No Kid Hungry campaign. She would also go on to partner with Save With Stories, a collaboration between No Kid Hungry and Save the Children, to read stories on Instagram for children out of school due to the COVID-19 pandemic.

After Australia's bushfires in 2020, Pink donated $500,000 to local fire services. Later in 2020, following her recovery from COVID-19, Pink donated one-million dollars to aid in combating the pandemic. The donation was split between the City of Los Angeles Mayor's Emergency COVID-19 Crisis Fund and the Temple University Hospital Fund in Philadelphia.

In July 2021, Pink offered to pay fines imposed on the Norwegian women's beach handball team after they wore shorts, like their male counterparts, instead of bikini bottoms. Also, in support of female empowerment, in 2022, Pink announced that all proceeds from 'Irrelevant' would be donated to Michelle Obama's non-partisan voting initiative, When We All Vote.

In April 2023, Pink received the National Champion Award from No Kid Hungry for her contributions and commitment to the campaign to end childhood hunger in America. She and Kelly Clarkson helped raise $60,000 for No Kid Hungry and the Sweet Relief Musicians Fund by auctioning off unique art pieces that depicted their songs in sound waves. Additionally, Pink and her daughter collaborated with Williams Sonoma to design spatulas for the annual Tools For Change fundraising program by No Kid Hungry.

Also in 2023, Pink supported UNICEF during the North American leg of her Summer Carnival Tour by promoting the charity. QR codes were placed at all merchandise stands, allowing fans to purchase basic necessities and school supplies for children in need, furthering UNICEF USA's mission.

Pink has been a strong advocate for LGBT rights and a vocal supporter of same-sex marriage. Not only has she done this through both her music and other activities. In her 2006 song, 'Dear Mr. President,' she criticised then-President George Bush's stance on gay marriage, questioning how a father could hate his own daughter if she were gay. Pink also joined protests against Proposition 8, a proposition to ban gay marriage, marching in a rally in downtown Los Angeles in November 2008. Her activism led to recognition with the Ally For Equality Award at the Human Rights Campaign Dinner in 2010.

In a 2012 interview with *Gaydar Radio*, Pink expressed her hope for a future where sexual orientation is not a defining characteristic, saying, "I think that the best day will be when we no longer talk about being gay or straight – it's not a 'gay wedding,' it's just a 'wedding;' it's not a 'gay marriage,' it's just 'a marriage.'" That same year, she told *The Advocate* about her relationships with girlfriends in her twenties and emphasised that she doesn't define her sexual orientation, adding that she appreciates her lesbian and bisexual female fans.

In 2023, *Billboard* recognised 'Raise Your Glass' as one of the top LGBT Anthems of All Time. During an interview with *Gay Times*, Pink expressed that the queer community means "everything" to her, and she takes pride in being understood as an ally. She added that being understood for who she is and what she believes in is a significant part of her journey, saying, "We want to love, be loved, and be seen."

Pink also continues to be an ambassador for women. In 2017, she participated in the Women's March, a high-profile protest advocating for women's rights and equality. She attended the event with her family.

In recognition of her advocacy and charitable efforts, Pink received the People's Champion Award at the 2019 People's Choice Awards, acknowledging her involvement with multiple organisations and her commitment to making a positive impact.

An excellent advocate for mental health, at the MTV Video Music Awards in 2017, Pink demonstrated how she ensures to bring up her daughter with a healthy sense of self-esteem.

Upon picking up a Video Vanguard Award, Pink dedicated much of her acceptance speech to then six-year-old daughter Willow.

"Mama, I'm the ugliest girl I know," Pink recalled of what her daughter had told her. "I look like a boy with long hair."

Pink spoke of how it had worried her that Willow had expressed such a negative thought about herself. Explaining that after an initial feeling of anger and frustration, questioning which of Willow's schoolmates might have influenced her, Pink told of how she chose a calmer approach: she created a PowerPoint presentation for Willow, featuring "androgynous" singers who "live their truth." The presentation included Annie Lennox, Freddie Mercury, Michael Jackson, David Bowie, and Elton John, the aim being to illustrate diversity and acceptance to Willow.

Pink relayed the conversation that she went on to initiate with Willow, "When people make fun of me... do you see me growing my hair? 'No, Mama.' Do you see me changing my body? 'No Mama.' Do you see me selling out arenas all over the world? 'Yes, Mama.'"

As the crowd applauded, Pink concluded her speech with heartfelt words, expressing gratitude to the other artists present. She then addressed Willow, saying, "You, my darling girl, are beautiful. And I love you."

Pink's speech resonated with audiences around the world, revealing her commitment to combating harmful beauty standards and encouraging body positivity. As an ambassador for good mental health, Pink's actions show that she takes her role as a public figure and a mother seriously, advocating for values that empower young people and challenge societal pressures.

Pink's reassurance to Willow that she isn't ugly underscores a message of unconditional love and acceptance. In a world where young people, particularly girls, are constantly exposed to unrealistic beauty standards, Pink's affirmation to her daughter serves as a powerful counter-narrative. By telling Willow that beauty comes in all shapes and forms, Pink demonstrates the importance of instilling self-worth and confidence in children.

Pink's response to Willow's concerns also challenges societal norms that often equate beauty with conformity. By publicly addressing this issue, Pink brought attention to the pressures young people face to fit a certain mould. In her speech, when she emphasised that "we take the gravel in the shell and make a pearl," it encourages everyone to embrace their uniqueness and reject societal pressures to look a certain way. This message is crucial in a culture where beauty ideals can lead to negative body image and mental health issues.

Pink's effort to promote self-esteem and body confidence in a public sphere shows her commitment to creating a healthier environment for not just young people, but everyone. She used her platform to set a positive example for parents and guardians everywhere, raising awareness and seeking to inspire change.

Pink is passionate about animal rights. In 2003, she declined an invitation to perform at Prince William's twenty-first birthday party due to the Royal Family's controversial stance on hunting. A prominent supporter of PETA, she has used her platform to protest against KFC's treatment of animals and to criticise the Australian wool industry for its use of mulesing – a practice in which chunks of flesh are cut from lambs' hindquarters with shears to prevent flystrike, a condition caused by breeding them to produce excessive amounts of wool.

In 2007, Pink admitted that PETA had misled her about mulesing, leading her to state that she should have conducted more thorough research before supporting the campaign. Despite this, she continued to champion animal rights, headlining a concert called PAW (Party for Animals Worldwide) in Cardiff, Wales, in August 2007. By May 2008, Pink was officially recognised as an advocate for RSPCA Australia.

The singer joined comedian Ricky Gervais in PETA's Stolen For Fashion campaign against wearing fur and animal skins. In 2014, Pink expressed opposition to carriage riding in New York City. In 2013, she questioned Queen Elizabeth II about why the bear fur used for the Guards' caps hadn't been replaced with synthetic, cruelty-free material. Pink posed nude for PETA's I'd Rather Go

Naked Than Wear Fur campaign in 2015 and spoke out against SeaWorld in 2018 for keeping marine animals in confined spaces where all they could do was "swim in endless circles."

Pink's advocacy and charity work reveal that time and time again, she has used her platform as a vehicle through which she can help others. Her commitment to various social causes and her consistent support for charitable organisations demonstrate a deep sense of compassion and a desire to make a positive impact. This dedication to using her fame for good is a sign of a person with integrity, reinforcing Pink's reputation as an artist who cares about more than just her own success.

Pink has used her voice to raise awareness and push for change. She has participated in campaigns, spoken at events, and supported legislation that aligns with her values. This level of activism reflects Pink's genuine concern for societal issues and her willingness to use her platform to advocate for those whose voices might not otherwise be heard. Pink doesn't just talk about change; she actively participates in it. This approach to philanthropy and advocacy sets a positive example for her fans and fellow artists, demonstrating that fame can be used as a force for good.

Glitter in the Air - *The Evolution of Pink*

CHAPTER FOURTEEN
A LEGACY CREATED, A BRIGHT FUTURE AHEAD

During the earlier days of her career, Pink quickly became a standout in the music industry, praised by critics for her bold personality, distinctive style, and powerful vocals. Her debut album, *Can't Take Me Home*, introduced her as an artist with a unique edge and a rebellious spirit that set her apart from her pop contemporaries. Critics were impressed by her ability to blend pop with rock and R&B elements, while her raw and unapologetic attitude added a refreshing layer of authenticity to her music. This early acclaim marked the beginning of a successful career, built on Pink's talent and willingness to defy industry norms.

Early singles, such as 'There You Go' and 'Most Girls,' demonstrated her flair for catchy hooks and bold lyrics, earning her a loyal fan base. Critics noted that Pink brought a sense of authenticity to her music, with a fearless attitude that resonated with listeners. Her ability to blend pop with rock-infused energy and soulful elements garnered praise, signalling the arrival of an artist with a unique perspective and a bright future.

Pink would go on to be credited with breaking boundaries and pushing the envelope throughout her career. In 2003, the *Los Angeles Times* noted that Pink "stood up for her music, broke the music industry's mould, and scored a breakout hit, challenging a school of teen singers to find their own sounds."

In 2009, the same publication would describe Pink as a "powerhouse vocalist," noting her unique blend of rebellion, emotional rawness, humour, and "infectious" dance beats, which set a template for other pop divas like Katy Perry, Kesha, and

Rihanna. The same year, MTV described Pink as being a "fabulously fearless pop artist" who can "out-sing almost anyone out there. She can out-crazy Gaga or Lily. She's the total pop-star package, everything you'd want in a singer/entertainer/icon. And still, she remains oddly off the radar. Such is the price of busting borders."

Years later, Pink continues to receive similar praise for her music and personality as she progresses in her career. Her ability to evolve while maintaining her signature style has kept her relevant and respected in the industry, with critics commending her willingness to tackle personal themes and address social issues. Pink's capacity to connect with her audience through powerful anthems and emotional ballads has consistently reinforced her status as a dynamic and enduring artist.

While Pink has gained immense popularity and critical acclaim throughout her career, not everyone has always liked her work. Despite this, she has consistently shown an ability to stay true to herself, refusing to be deterred by criticism or negative feedback.

Pink's resilience in the face of criticism is a testament to her strength as an artist and her determination to carve out her own path. Her ability to withstand scrutiny and remain authentic has become a defining trait, earning her respect and admiration. "You can do anything and there will be someone who doesn't like it," she told *The Guardian* in 2014. "That's the way the world is now. We've lost our manners and, unfortunately, what people don't realise is that by being that way, they're losing the joy in their lives and the opportunity to be pleasantly surprised."

Contradictorily, despite talking about manners, she also said, "I love pop music," adding, "I like flying around on stage. I have such a good time. People say, 'Why's she always in the fucking air?' Because I'm having more fun than you, fuck you."

As Pink's career has evolved, so has her versatility as an artist. Critics have praised her ability to experiment with different genres and collaborate with a wide range of musicians. This adaptability has allowed Pink to explore new musical territories while staying true to her roots, resulting in albums that are both innovative and accessible. Critics appreciate her fearless approach to songwriting; her addressing of themes of empowerment, relationships, and personal growth with a level of authenticity that resonates with fans. This versatility and fearlessness have been recurring themes in the praise she receives.

Pink's personality continues to be a focal point of critical acclaim. Her outspoken nature sets her apart from other pop artists, earning her admiration and respect. Critics often highlight Pink's role as a positive influence, with her refusal to conform to industry stereotypes and her advocacy for social justice issues. Her willingness to speak openly about her experiences and struggles adds depth to her music and reinforces her position as a role model.

Pink's live performances have also been a consistent source of praise throughout her career. Critics commend her high-energy shows, intricate stage setups, and daring acrobatics, which have become hallmarks of her concerts. Pink's commitment to delivering unforgettable live experiences reinforces her reputation as one of the industry's top performers. The consistency of her live performances, combined with her captivating stage presence, has earned her accolades from critics and fans alike, demonstrating that her talent and charisma are enduring.

With nine Pink-branded studio albums under her belt, it is interesting to consider what Pink will do next. As an artist known for her versatility and fearless approach to music, she has continually evolved throughout her career. Her trajectory has been anything but predictable, which is part of what makes the prospect of her next move so intriguing. Pink's adaptability suggests that her next project could take any number of directions, and it's this unpredictability that keeps fans and critics alike eagerly anticipating.

Given Pink's history of exploring various musical genres, it's likely that her future work will continue to push boundaries. She has ventured into pop, rock, folk, and even country elements, each time adding her unique flair. Her willingness to experiment suggests that her next album could feature unexpected sounds and influences.

Whether it's returning to her pop rock roots or exploring entirely new territory, Pink's capacity for musical exploration has the scope to open up a world of possibilities. Given Pink's evolving perspective on life and her ongoing activism, her future work could delve even deeper into personal and societal themes, all of which are likely to continue to attract the attention and support of her fans. Also, based on the number of artists Pink has collaborated with throughout her career, it's likely that by seeking out new partnerships, she may further expand her musical range, introducing her fans to fresh sounds and perspectives.

As Pink's career progresses, she balances her music with her personal life, including her role as a mother and advocate for social causes. This balance between the demands of a successful career and personal responsibilities could influence her future work, inspiring further themes of resilience, growth, and family.

Pink's ability to navigate life's complexities with grace and authenticity adds a relatable dimension to her music, suggesting that her next project could be as personal as it is powerful.

With a career defined by evolution and reinvention, Pink's future work could explore new musical territories, address personal and societal themes, and feature exciting collaborations. Her ongoing journey as an artist and individual makes the prospect of her next project an exciting and intriguing one, leaving fans and critics ready to embrace and welcome her next chapter.

DISCOGRAPHY
Studio Albums

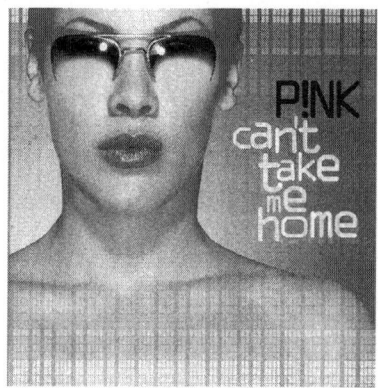

Can't Take Me Home (2000)

1. Split Personality
(written by Alecia Moore, Terence "Tramp-Baby" Abney, Kenneth "Babyface" Edmonds) (produced by Babyface, Abney, Daryl Simmons)

2. Hell wit Ya
(written by Moore, Kevin "She'kspere" Briggs, Kandi Burruss, Darius Green)
(produced by Briggs, Burruss)

3. Most Girls
(written by Edmonds, Damon Thomas)
(produced by Babyface)

4. There You Go
(written by Moore, Briggs, Burruss)
(produced by Briggs, Burruss)

5. You Make Me Sick
(written by Obi Nwobosi, Ainsworth Prasad, Marthony Tabb)
(produced by Babyface, Anthony President, Brainz Dimilo)

6. Let Me Let You Know
(written by Neal Creque, Sean Hall, Christopher "Tricky" Stewart, Robin Thicke) (produced by Tricky, Hall)

7. Love Is Such A Crazy Thing
(written by Jason Boyd, Tionne "T-Boz" Watkins, Daron Jones, Michael Keith, Quinnes Parker, Marvin Scandrick, Lamont "Stro" Maxwell, Courtney Sills)
(produced by Lamont Maxwell, Jones)

8. Private Show
(written by Kenneth Karlin, Andrea Martin, Ivan Matias, Carsten "Soulshock" Schack) (produced by Soulshock & Karlin)

9. Can't Take Me Home
(written by Moore, Harold Frasier, Steve "Rhythm" Clarke)
(produced by The Specialists, Clarke)

10. Stop Falling
(written by Moore, Will Baker, Pete Woodruff)
(produced by Will & Pete)

11. Do What U Do
(written by James Hollins, Ezekiel Lewis, Kawan Prather, Maurice "Big Reese" Sinclair) (produced by P.A.)

12. Hiccup
(written by Moore, Rozonda "Chilli" Thomas, Tionne Watkins, Harold Frasier, Delouie Avant, Steve "Rhythm" Clarke)
(produced by The Specialists, Clarke)

13. Is It Love
(written by Moore, Frasier, Avant, Clarke, Aaron Philips)
(produced by Clarke, Pink)

UK special edition and digital expanded edition bonus tracks:
14. There You Go (Sovereign Mix)
15. Most Girls (X-Men Vocal Mix)

Discography

Missundaztood (2001)

1. Missundaztood
(written by Moore, Linda Perry)
(produced by Perry, Damon Elliott)

2. Don't Let Me Get Me
(written by Moore, Dallas Austin)
(produced by Austin)

3. Just Like A Pill
(written by Moore, Austin)
(produced by Austin)

4. Get The Party Started
(written by Perry)
(produced by Perry)

5. Respect (featuring Scratch)
(written by Moore, Perry)
(produced by Perry, Elliott)

6. 18 Wheeler
(written by Moore, Austin)
(produced by Austin)

7. Family Portrait
(written by Moore, Scott Storch)
(produced by Storch)

8. Misery (featuring Steven Tyler)
(written by Richie Supa)
(produced by Marti Frederiksen, Supa)

9. Dear Diary
(written by Moore, Perry)
(produced by Perry)

10. Eventually
(written by Moore, Perry)
(produced by Perry)

11. Lonely Girl (featuring Linda Perry)
(written by Perry)
(produced by Perry)

12. Numb
(written by Moore, Austin)
(produced by Austin)

13. Gone To California
(written by Moore, Perry)
(produced by Perry, Elliott)

14. My Vietnam
(written by Moore, Perry)
(produced by Perry, Elliott)

International edition bonus track:
15. Catch-22
(written by Moore and Perry)
(produced by Perry and Elliott)

Discography

Try This (2003)

1\. Trouble
(written by Moore, Tim Armstrong)
(produced by Armstrong, John Fields)

2\. God Is A DJ
(written by Moore, Billy Mann, Jonathan S. Davis)
(produced by Mann, Davis)

3\. Last To Know
(written by Moore, Armstrong)
(produced by Armstrong)

4\. Tonight's The Night
(written by Moore, Armstrong)
(produced by Armstrong)

5\. Oh My God (featuring Peaches)
(written by Moore, Armstrong, Merrill Nisker)
(produced by Armstrong)

6\. Catch Me While I'm Sleeping
(written by Moore, Linda Perry)
(produced by Perry, Fields)

7\. Waiting For Love
(written by Moore, Perry, Eric Schermerhorn, Paul Ill, Brian MacLeod)
(produced by Perry)

8\. Save My Life
(written by Moore, Armstrong)
(produced by Armstrong)

9\. Try Too Hard
(written by Moore, Perry)
(produced by Perry, Fields)

10\. Humble Neighborhoods
(written by Moore, Armstrong)
(produced by Armstrong, Fields)

11. Walk Away
(written by Moore, Armstrong)
(produced by Armstrong)

12. Unwind
(written by Moore, Armstrong)
(produced by Armstrong)

13. Love Song
(written by Moore, Damon Elliott)
(produced by Elliott)

14. Hooker (hidden track)
(written by Moore, Armstrong)
(produced by Armstrong)

International version:
13. Feel Good Time (featuring William Orbit)
(by William Orbit, Beck Hansen, Jay Ferguson)
(produced by Orbit)

14. Love Song
15. Hooker (hidden track)

I'm Not Dead (2006)

1. Stupid Girls
(written by Moore, Billy Mann, Nikey Olovson, Robin Lynch)
(produced by Mann, MachoPsycho)

2. Who Knew
(written by Moore, Max Martin, Lukasz Gottwald)
(produced by Martin, Dr. Luke)

3. Long Way To Happy
(written by Moore, Butch Walker)
(produced by Walker)

4. Nobody Knows
(written by Moore, Mann)
(produced by Mann)

5. Dear Mr. President (featuring Indigo Girls)
(written by Moore, Mann)
(produced by Mann, Moore)

6. I'm Not Dead
(written by Moore, Mann)
(produced by Al Clay, Mann)

7. 'Cuz I Can
(written by Moore, Martin, Gottwald)
(produced by Martin, Dr. Luke)

8. Leave Me Alone (I'm Lonely)
(written by Moore, Walker)
(produced by Walker)

9. U + Ur Hand
(written by Moore, Martin, Gottwald, Rami)
(produced by Martin, Dr. Luke)

10. Runaway
(written by Moore, Mann)
(produced by Josh Abraham, Mann)

11. The One That Got Away
(written by Moore, Mann)
(produced by Mann, Moore)

12. I Got Money Now
(written by Moore, Mike Elizondo)
(produced by Elizondo)

13. Conversations with My 13 Year Old Self
(written by Moore, Mann)
(produced by Mann)

14. I Have Seen The Rain (featuring Jim Moore) (hidden track) (written by Jim Moore)
(produced by Moore)

International bonus track:
14. Fingers
(written by Moore, Mann)
(produced by Mann, Chris Rojas)

15. I Have Seen The Rain (featuring Jim Moore) (hidden track)

UK bonus tracks:
14. Fingers
15. Centerfold
(written by Moore, Cathy Dennis, Greg Kurstin)
(produced by Kurstin)

16. I Have Seen The Rain (featuring Jim Moore) (hidden track)

iTunes Store bonus tracks:
15. Crash & Burn
(written by Moore, Mann)
(produced by Mann, Chris Rojas)

16. Centerfold
17. Fingers

Australian tour edition bonus tracks:
14. Fingers
15. I Have Seen The Rain (featuring James T. Moore)
16. Who Knew (Bimbo Jones Radio Edit)
17. U + Ur Hand (Beatcult Remix)

Platinum edition bonus tracks:
15. Heartbreaker
(written by Moore, Kara DioGuardi, Greg Wells)
16. Centerfold
17. Fingers
18. U + Ur Hand" (Bimbo Jones Remix)

Discography

Funhouse (2008)

1. So What
(written by Alecia Moore, Max Martin, Shellback)
(produced by Martin)

2. Sober
(written by Moore, Nathaniel Hills, Kara DioGuardi, Marcella Araica)
(produced by Danja, Tony Kanal, Jimmy Harry)

3. I Don't Believe You
(written by Moore, Martin)
(produced by Martin)

4. One Foot Wrong
(written by Moore, Francis White)
(produced by Eg White)

5. Please Don't Leave Me
(written by Moore, Martin)
(produced by Martin)

6. Bad Influence
(written by Moore, Billy Mann, Butch Walker, Robin Lynch, Niklas Olovson)
(produced by Mann, Walker, MachoPsycho)

7. Funhouse
(written by Moore, Tony Kanal, Jimmy Harry)
(produced by Kanal, Jimmy Harry)

8. Crystal Ball
(written by Moore, Mann)
(produced by Mann)

9. Mean
(written by Moore, Walker)
(produced by Walker)

10. It's All Your Fault
(written by Moore, Martin, Shellback)
(produced by Martin)

11. Ave Mary A
(written by Moore, Mann, Pete Wallace)
(produced by Mann, Al Clay, Wallace)

12. Glitter In The Air
(written by Moore, Mann)
(produced by Mann)

International edition and German Tchibo special edition bonus track:
13. This Is How It Goes Down (featuring Travis McCoy)
(written by Moore, Walker)
(produced by Walker)

Tour edition bonus track:
14. Push You Away
(written by Moore, Walker)
(produced by Walker)

UK and Japan edition bonus tracks:
14. Boring
(written by Moore, Martin, Shellback)
(produced by Martin)

15. So What (music video)

American digital deluxe edition bonus tracks:
13. Why Did I Ever Like You
(written by Moore, Greg Wells)
(produced by Wells)

14. Could've Had Everything
(written by Moore, White)
(produced by White)

15. So What (music video) (iTunes Store only)

16. This Is How It Goes Down (featuring Travis McCoy) (iTunes Store pre-order only)

Discography

The Truth About Love (2012)

1. Are We All We Are
(written by Moore, Butch Walker, John Hill, Emile Haynie)
(produced by Walker, Hill, Haynie)

2. Blow Me (One Last Kiss)
(written by Moore, Greg Kurstin)
(produced by Kurstin)

3. Try
(written by Busbee, Ben West)
(produced by Kurstin)

4. Just Give Me A Reason (featuring Nate Ruess)
(written by Moore, Ruess, Jeff Bhasker)
(produced by Bhasker)

5. True Love (featuring Lily Allen)
(written by Moore, Allen, Kurstin)
(produced by Kurstin)

6. How Come You're Not Here?
(written by Moore, Kurstin)
(produced by Kurstin)

7. Slut Like You
(written by Moore, Max Martin, Shellback)
(produced by Martin, Shellback)

8. The Truth About Love
(written by Moore, Billy Mann, David Schuler)
(produced by Mann, Schuler)

9. Beam Me Up
(written by Moore, Mann)
(produced by Mann)

10. Walk Of Shame
(written by Moore, Kurstin)
(produced by Kurstin)

11. Here Comes The Weekend (featuring Eminem)
(written by Moore, Khalil Abdul Rahman, Pranam Injeti, Erik Alcock, Liz Rodrigues, Marshall Mathers)
(produced by DJ Khalil, Chin Injeti, John Brown)

12. Where Did The Beat Go?
(written by Moore, Mann, Jon Keep, Steve Daly)
(produced by Mann, Tracklacers)

13. The Great Escape
(written by Moore, Dan Wilson)
(produced by Wilson)

US and Canadian iTunes Store edition bonus tracks:
14. Chaos & Piss
(written by Moore, Francis White)
(produced by Eg White)

15. Timebomb
(written by Moore, Kurstin)
(produced by Kurstin)

US Target and international deluxe edition bonus tracks:
14. My Signature Move
(written by Moore, Walker, Jake Sinclair)
(produced by Walker)

15. Is This Thing On?
(written by Moore, Walker, Sinclair)
(produced by Walker)

16. Run
(written by Moore, Walker, Sinclair)
(produced by Walker)

17. Good Old Days
(written by Moore, Mann, Schuler)
(produced by Mann, Schuler)

Japanese edition bonus track:
18. The King Is Dead But The Queen Is Alive
(written by Moore, Mann, Walker, Niklas "Nikey" Olovson, Robin Lynch)
(produced by Mann, Machopsycho, Walker)

International iTunes Store deluxe edition bonus tracks:
18. Chaos & Piss
19. Timebomb

Fan edition bonus track:
20. The King Is Dead But The Queen Is Alive

Discography

Beautiful Trauma (2017)

1. Beautiful Trauma
(written by Alecia Moore, Jack Antonoff)
(produced by Antonoff)

2. Revenge (featuring Eminem)
(written by Moore, Marshall Mathers, Max Martin, Shellback)
(produced by Shellback, Martin)

3. Whatever You Want
(written by Moore, Martin, Shellback)
(produced by Shellback, Martin)

4. What About Us
(written by Moore, Johnny McDaid, Steve McCutcheon)
(produced by Steve Mac)

5. But We Lost It
(written by Moore, Greg Kurstin)
(produced by Kurstin)

6. Barbies
(written by Moore, Julia Michaels, Ross Golan, Jakob Jerlström, Ludvig Söderberg)
(produced by The Struts, Golan)

7. Where We Go
(written by Moore, Kurstin)
(produced by Kurstin)

8. For Now
(written by Moore, Michaels, Mattias Larsson, Robin Fredriksson, Martin)
(produced by Mattman & Robin)

9. Secrets
(written by Moore, Martin, Shellback, Oscar Holter)
(produced by Shellback, Martin, Holter)

10. Better Life
(written by Moore, Antonoff, Sam Dew)
(produced by Antonoff)

11. I Am Here
(written by Moore, Billy Mann, Christian Medice)
(produced by Mann, Medice)

12. Wild Hearts Can't Be Broken
(written by Moore, Michael Busbee)
(produced by Busbee)

13. You Get My Love
(written by Moore, Tobias Jesso Jr.)
(produced by Moore, Jesso Jr.)

Japanese CD bonus track:
14. White Rabbit
(written by Grace Slick)
(produced by Andy Dodd.John Volaitis)

Discography

Hurts 2B Human (2019)

1. Hustle
(written by Alecia Moore, Dan Reynolds, Jorgen Odegard)
(produced by Odegard, Reynolds)

2. (Hey Why) Miss You Sometime
(written by Moore, Max Martin, Shellback)
(produced by Shellback, Martin)

3. Walk Me Home
(written by Moore, Scott Harris, Nate Ruess)
(produced by Peter Thomas, Kyle Moorman)

4. My Attic
(written by Julia Michaels, Ilsey Juber, Freddy Wexler)

(produced by The Struts, Freddy Wexler)

5. 90 Days (featuring Wrabel)
(written by Moore, Wrabel, Steve Robson)
(produced by Robson, Wrabel, Simon Gooding)

6. Hurts 2B Human (featuring Khalid)
(written by Moore, Teddy Geiger, Harris, Anna-Catherine Hartley, Alexander "Xplicit" Izquierdo, Khalid Robinson)
(produced by Odegard)

7. Can We Pretend (featuring Cash Cash)
(written by Moore, Ryan Tedder, Jean Paul Makhlouf, Alex Makhlouf, Samuel Frisch)
(produced by Cash Cash, Tedder)

8. Courage
(written by Moore, Greg Kurstin, Sia Furler)
(produced by Kurstin)

9. Happy
(written by Moore, Geiger, Alexandra Yatchenko, Steph Jones)
(produced by Oscar Görres, Geiger)

10. We Could Have It All
(written by Moore, Kurstin, Beck Hansen)
(produced by Kurstin)

11. Love Me Anyway (featuring Chris Stapleton)
(written by Moore, Allen Shamblin, Tom Douglas)
(produced by Moore, Sal Oliverim Simon Gooding)

12. Circle Game
(written by Moore, Kurstin)
(produced by Kurstin)

13. The Last Song Of Your Life
(written by Moore, Billy Mann)
(produced by Mann, Moore)

Japanese bonus track:
14. More
(written by Moore, Jetta John-Hartley, Busbee)
(produced by Busbee)

Discography

Trustfall (2023)

1. When I Get There
(written by Amy Wadge, David Hodges)
(produced by Hodges)

2. Trustfall
(written by Moore, Johnny McDaid, Fred Gibson)
(produced by McDaid, Fred, Graham Archer)

3. Turbulence
(written by Matthew Koma, Madison Love)
(produced by Koma)

4. Long Way To Go (featuring The Lumineers)
(written by Moore, Jeremiah Fraites, Jesse Shatkin, John Stephen Sudduth, Maureen "Mozella" McDonald, Wesley Schultz)
(produced by Moore, Fraites, Shatkin, Schultz, Simon Gooding, David Baron)

5. Kids In Love (featuring First Aid Kit)
(written by Ludvig Söderberg, Jakob Jerlström, Klara Söderberg)
(produced by A Strut)

6. Never Gonna Not Dance Again
(written by Moore, Max Martin, Shellback)
(produced by Martin, Shellback)

7. Runaway
(written by Edvard Erfjord, Clementine Douglas)
(produced by Greg Kurstin)

8. Last Call
(written by Moore, Billy Mann, Pete Wallace)
(produced by Mann, Wallace)

9. Hate Me
(written by Moore, Kurstin)
(produced by Kurstin)

10. Lost Cause
(written by Wrabel, Sam de Jong, Sam Romans)
(produced by Moore, de Jong)

11. Feel Something
(written by Teddy Geiger, Ian Franzino, Jason Evigan, Nate Mercereau)
(produced by Geiger, Evigan, Mercereau, Afterhrs)

12. Our Song
(written by Shatkin, Jessica Karpov, McDonald)
(produced by Shatkin, Harloe)

13. Just Say I'm Sorry (featuring Chris Stapleton)
(written by Moore, Chris Stapleton)
(produced by Kurstin)

Japanese edition bonus track:
14. Never Gonna Not Dance Again (Sam Feldt remix)
(written by Moore, Martin, Shellback)
(produced by Martin, Shellback, Sam Feldt)

Collaborative album:

Rose Ave. by You+Me (2014)
(All tracks written by Dallas Green and Alecia Moore except where noted)
(All tracks produced by Dallas Green and Alecia Moore)

1. Capsized
2. From A Closet In Norway (Oslo Blues)
3. Gently
4. Love Gone Wrong
5. You And Me
6. Unbeliever
7. Second Guess
8. Break The Cycle
9. Open Door
10. No Ordinary Love (Sade Adu, Stuart Matthewman)

GIGOGRAPHY

Party Tour 2002

2nd May	Web Theatre, Phoenix, US
4th May	AVA Amphitheatre, Tucson, US
5th May	Rain in the Desert, Las Vegas, US
7th May	Kingsbury Hall, Salt Lake City, US
9th May	Fillmore Auditorium, Denver, US
10th May	Cheenh Lounge, Bernalillo, US
12th May	Austin Music Hall, Austin, US
14th May	Verizon Wireless Theatre, Houston, US
15th May	NextStage Performance Theatre, Grand Prairie, US
18th May	Hard Rock Live, Orlando, US
19th May	Au-Rene Theatre, Fort Lauderdale, US
22nd May	The Tabernacle, Atlanta, US
25th May	Star Pavilion, Hershey, US
26th May	Oakdale Theatre, Wallingford, US
28th May	Beacon Theatre, New York City, US
29th May	Beacon Theatre, New York City, US
31st May	Orpheum Theatre, Boston, US
1st June	Tower Theatre, Upper Darby, US
2nd June	Giants Stadium, East Rutherford, US
4th June	Nation, Washington, D.C., US
5th June	Tower City Amphitheatre, Cleveland, US
7th June	I.C. Light Amphitheatre, Pittsburgh, US
9th June	Massey Hall, Toronto, Canada
10th June	State Theatre, Detroit, US
12th June	Rosemont Theatre, Rosemont, US
13th June	Orpheum Theatre, Minneapolis, US
15th June	Rose Bowl, Pasadena, US
18th June	Spokane Opera House, Spokane, US
19th June	Orpheum Theatre, Vancouver, Canada
22nd June	Theatre of Clouds, Portland, US
24th June	Ruth Finley Person Theatre, Santa Rosa, US
25th June	Warfield Theatre, San Francisco, US
28th June	Wiltern Theatre, Los Angeles, US
29th June	Wiltern Theatre, Los Angeles, US
30th June	San Diego County Fair Grandstand, San Diego, US

Lenny Kravitz Tour 2002

12th July	Verizon Wireless Amphitheatre, Virginia Beach, Virginia, US
13th July	Trump Taj Mahal Atlantic City, New Jersey, US
16th July	Jiffy Lube Live, Bristow, Virginia, US*
17th July	PNC Bank Arts Centre, Holmdel, New Jersey, US
19th July	Jones Beach Theatre, Wantagh, New York, US
20th July	Tweeter Centre, Mansfield, Massachusetts, US*
22nd July	Blossom Music Centre, Cuyahoga Falls, Ohio, US
23rd July	DTE Energy Music Theatre, Clarkston, Michigan, US
24th July	Blossom Music Centre, Cuyahoga Falls, Ohio, US*
26th July	Tweeter Centre, Tinley Park, Illinois, US
27th July	Verizon Wireless Music Centre, Noblesville, Indiana, US*
30th July	Budweiser Stage, Ontario Place, Toronto, Ontario, Canada
2nd August	Polaris Amphitheatre, Columbus, Ohio, US
4th August	Molson Amphitheatre, Toronto, Canada*
5th August	Xfinity Centre, Mansfield, Massachusetts, US
8th August	Cellairis Amphitheatre, Atlanta, Georgia, US*
9th August	Starwood Amphitheatre, Nashville, Tennessee, US
10th August	iTHINK Financial Amphitheatre, West Palm Beach, Florida, US

11th August	Ice Palace, Tampa, Florida, US
15th August	Starplex Ampitheater/ Smirnoff, Dallas, Texas, US
17th August	Cynthia Woods Mitchell Pavilion, The Woodlands, Texas, US*
18th August	Verizon Wireless Amphitheatre, San Antonio, Texas, US*
20th August	Journal Pavilion, Albuquerque, New Mexico, US*
21st August	Fiddler's Green Amphitheatre, Greenwood Village, Colorado, US*
22nd August	The Gorge Amphitheatre, George, Washington, US*
23rd August	The Gorge Amphitheatre, George, Washington, US*
24th August	General Motors Place, Vancouver, British Columbia, Canada
26th August	Shoreline Amphitheatre, Mountain View, California, US
27th August	Irvine Meadows Amphitheatre, Irvine, California, US
29th August	Auto West Amphitheatre, Sacramento, California, US*
31st August	Mandalay Bay Resort & Casino, Las Vegas, Nevada, US
1st September	North Island Credit Union Amphitheatre, Chula Vista, California, US
2nd September	Cricket Pavilion, Phoenix, Arizona, US
7th September	Estadio Azteca, Mexico City, Mexico
13th September	AmSouth Amphitheatre, Nashville, Tennessee, US*
14th September	Verizon Wireless Music Centre, Noblesville, Indiana, US
16th September	Budweiser Stage, Ontario Place, Toronto, Ontario, Canada

* Unconfirmed if Pink performed at these shows.

Party Tour 2002

5th November	Manchester Apollo, Manchester, England
6th November	Point Theatre, Dublin, Ireland
8th November	E-Werk, Cologne, Germany
11th November	Carling Academy, Birmingham, England
12th November	O2 Brixton Academy, London, England
19th November	Kōsei Nenkin Kaikan, Osaka, Japan
21st November	Tokyo International Forum, Tokyo, Japan
22nd November	Public Hall, Shibuya, Japan
26th November	Dunedin Town Hall, Dunedin, New Zealand
27th November	Westpac Centre, Christchurch, New Zealand
29th November	Queens Wharf Events Centre, Wellington, New Zealand
30th November	Western Springs Stadium, Auckland, New Zealand
3rd December	Subiaco Oval, Perth, Australia
6th December	Adelaide Oval, Adelaide, Australia
8th December	Telstra Dome, Melbourne, Australia
10th December	Twin Towns S Club, Gold Coast, Australia
11th December	ANZ Stadium, Brisbane, Australia
12th December	Entertainment Centre, Wollongong, Australia
14th December	Telstra Stadium, Sydney, Australia
18th December	Blaisdell Arena, Honolulu, US

Try This Tour 2004

19th February	Point Theatre, Dublin, Ireland
20th February	Odyssey Arena, Belfast, Northern Ireland
23rd February	Forest National, Brussels, Belgium
25th February	Preussag Arena, Hanover, Germany
27th February	Hanns-Martin-Schleyer-Halle, Stuttgart, Germany
28th February	Hallenstadion, Zürich, Switzerland
29th February	Hallenstadion, Zürich, Switzerland
2nd March	Festhalle Frankfurt, Frankfurt, Germany
4th March	Olympiahalle, Munich, Germany
5th March	Arena Leipzig, Leipzig, Germany
7th March	Max-Schmeling-Halle, Berlin, Germany
8th March	Forum Copenhagen, Copenhagen, Denmark
10th March	Oslo Spektrum, Oslo, Norway
11th March	Hovet, Stockholm, Sweden
13th March	Color Line Arena, Hamburg, Germany
15th March	Kölnarena, Cologne, Germany

Gigography

17th March	Palais Omnisports de Paris-Bercy, Paris, France
18th March	Sportpaleis van Ahoy, Rotterdam, Netherlands
20th March	NEC Arena, Birmingham, England
21st March	Nottingham Arena, Nottingham, England
23rd March	Wembley Arena, London, England
24th March	Wembley Arena, London, England
26th March	Manchester Evening News Arena, Manchester, England
27th March	Hallam FM Arena, Sheffield, England
28th March	The Ritz, Manchester, England
30th March	Telewest Arena, Newcastle, England
31st March	Scottish Exhibition Centre, Hall 4, Glasgow, Scotland
1st April	Scottish Exhibition Centre, Hall 4, Glasgow, Scotland
4th April	Wiener Stadthalle, Vienna, Austria
5th April	Budapest Sports Arena, Budapest, Hungary
8th April	Olympiahalle, Munich, Germany
10th April	König Pilsener Arena, Oberhausen, Germany
24th April	Newcastle Entertainment Centre, Newcastle, Australia
25th April	Sydney Entertainment Centre, Sydney, Australia
28th April	Brisbane Entertainment Centre, Brisbane, Australia
30th April	Challenge Stadium, Perth, Australia
3rd May	Adelaide Entertainment Centre, Adelaide, Australia
5th May	Rod Laver Arena, Melbourne, Australia
26th June	Grosse Allmend, Frauenfeld, Switzerland
27th June	Stade Jos Haupert, Niederkorn, Luxembourg
29th June	Heineken Music Hall, Amsterdam, Netherlands
1st July	Werchter Festival Grounds, Werchter, Belgium
2nd July	Kościuszki Square, Gdynia, Poland
6th July	Olimpiysky, Moscow, Russia
7th July	Ice Palace, Saint Petersburg, Russia
9th July	Storgatan, Sundsvall, Sweden
10th July	Balado, Kinross, Scotland
11th July	Punchestown Racecourse, Naas, Ireland
14th July	Messegelände Balingen, Balingen, Germany
16th July	Samsung Arena, Bratislava, Slovakia
17th July	Schwarzl Freizeit Zentrum, Graz, Austria
20th July	Belgrade Fair – Hall 1, Belgrade, Serbia and Montenegro
22nd July	Piața Sfatului, Brașov, Romania
24th July	Solar Beach, Kilyos, Turkey
26th July	Auditorium di San Romano, Lucca, Italy
28th July	Théâtre Antique de Vienne, Vienne, France
29th July	La Pinède, Antibes, France
31st July	Velodrom, Berlin, Germany
1st August	Sazka Arena, Prague, Czech Republic
4th August	Freilichtbühne im Stadtpark, Hamburg, Germany
5th August	Skanderborg Lake, Skanderborg, Denmark
10th August	Laugardalshöll, Reykjavík, Iceland
13th August	Theatre du Parc Expo De Colmar, Colmar, France
14th August	Rock eau Rouge, St. Vith, Belgium
15th August	Ostseehalle, Kiel, Germany
17th August	Museumsplatz, Bonn, Germany
19th August	Festivalgelände am Rotten, Gampel, Switzerland
21st August	Hylands Park, Chelmsford, England
22nd August	Weston Park, Weston-under-Lizard, England

I'm Not Dead Tour 2006

27th June	Fillmore Auditorium, San Francisco, US
28th June	Avalon Theatre, Avalon, US
30th June	The Beach at Mandalay Bay, Las Vegas, US
5th July	First Avenue, Minneapolis, US
9th July	Vogue Theatre, Indianapolis, US
12th July	House of Blues, Cleveland, US
13th July	Kool Haus, Toronto, Canada

Glitter in the Air - *The Evolution of Pink*

15th July	Electric Factory, Philadelphia, US
16th July	9:30 Club, Washington, D.C., US
18th July	Avalon Ballroom, Boston, US
19th July	Webster Hall, New York City, US
21st July	House of Blues, Myrtle Beach, US
24th July	Revolution Live, Fort Lauderdale, US
25th July	Jannus Landing, St. Petersburg, US
26th July	House of Blues, Orlando, US
28th July	Warehouse Live, Houston, US
29th July	Gypsy Tea Room, Dallas, US
8th September	Park Orman, Istanbul, Turkey
9th September	Spiaggia del Faro, Jesolo, Italy
27th September	Hallenstadion, Zürich, Switzerland
28th September	Olympiahalle, Innsbruck, Austria
1st October	Sportpaleis, Antwerp, Belgium
3rd October	National Indoor Arena, Birmingham, England
4th October	Wembley Arena, London, England
7th October	Olympiahalle, Munich, Germany
8th October	Rothaus Arena, Freiburg, Germany
10th October	Max-Schmeling-Halle, Berlin, Germany
11th October	TUI Arena, Hanover, Germany
12th October	Nuremberg Arena, Nuremberg, Germany
14th October	Sportpaleis van Ahoy, Rotterdam, Netherlands
15th October	GO Planet, Enschede, Netherlands
18th October	Festhalle Frankfurt, Frankfurt, Germany
19th October	Kölnarena, Cologne, Germany
20th October	König Pilsener Arena, Oberhausen, Germany
22nd October	Arena Leipzig, Leipzig, Germany
23rd October	SAP Arena, Mannheim, Germany
25th October	Forum Copenhagen, Copenhagen, Denmark
27th October	Oslo Spektrum, Oslo, Norway
28th October	Hovet, Stockholm, Sweden
30th October	Helsinki Ice Hall, Helsinki, Finland
31st October	Saku Suurhall Arena, Tallinn, Estonia
1st November	Arena Riga, Riga, Latvia
5th November	Manchester Evening News Arena, Manchester, England
7th November	Cardiff International Arena, Cardiff, Wales
10th November	Metro Radio Arena, Newcastle, England
11th November	Trent FM Arena Nottingham, Nottingham, England
13th November	Plymouth Pavilions, Plymouth, England
14th November	Brighton Centre, Brighton, England
16th November	Point Theatre, Dublin, Ireland
17th November	Odyssey Arena, Belfast, Northern Ireland
18th November	Odyssey Arena, Belfast, Northern Ireland
20th November	Press & Journal Arena, Aberdeen, Scotland
21st November	Press & Journal Arena, Aberdeen, Scotland
23rd November	Scottish Exhibition Hall 4, Glasgow, Scotland
24th November	Scottish Exhibition Hall 4, Glasgow, Scotland
26th November	Brighton Centre, Brighton, England
27th November	Windsor Hall, Bournemouth, England
29th November	NEC Arena, Birmingham, England
30th November	Scottish Exhibition Centre, Glasgow, Scotland
2nd December	Hallam FM Arena, Sheffield, England
3rd December	Windsor Hall, Bournemouth, England
4th December	Wembley Arena, London, England
6th December	Heineken Music Hall, Amsterdam, Netherlands
7th December	Heineken Music Hall, Amsterdam, Netherlands
8th December	Hanns-Martin-Schleyer-Halle, Stuttgart, Germany
10th December	Wiener Stadthalle, Vienna, Austria
12th December	Color Line Arena, Hamburg, Germany
13th December	Sazka Arena, Prague, Czech Republic
15th December	Dražen Petrović Basketball Hall, Zagreb, Croatia
16th December	Salzburgarena, Salzburg, Austria
17th December	SEG Geneva Arena, Geneva, Switzerland
19th December	Palais Omnisports de Paris-Bercy, Paris, France

Gigography

20th December	Halle Tony Garnier, Lyon, France
21st December	Mazda Palace, Milan, Italy

Justin Timberlake FutureSex/LoveShow Tour 2007

8th January	iPayOne Centre, San Diego, US
9th January	Honda Centre, Anaheim, US
11th January	HP Pavilion, San Jose, US
12th January	ARCO Arena, Sacramento, US
14th January	Jobing.com Arena, Glendale, US
30th January	Air Canada Centre, Toronto, Canada
31st January	Bell Centre, Montreal, Canada
27th February	Philips Arena, Atlanta, US
1st March	New Orleans Arena, New Orleans, US
4th March	Toyota Centre, Houston, US
5th March	American Airlines Centre, Dallas, US
8th March	Qwest Centre, Omaha, US
12th March	Rosemont, Allstate Arena, US
13th March	Rosemont, Allstate Arena, US
18th March	John Paul Jones Arena, Charlottesville, US
24th March	Mohegan Sun Arena, Uncasville, US
26th March	Verizon Wireless Arena, Manchester, US
27th March	Wachovia Centre, Philadelphia, US

I'm Not Dead Tour 2007

18th April	Challenge Stadium, Perth, Australia
19th April	Challenge Stadium, Perth, Australia
20th April	Challenge Stadium, Perth, Australia
22nd April	Adelaide Entertainment Centre, Adelaide, Australia
23rd April	Adelaide Entertainment Centre, Adelaide, Australia
26th April	Rod Laver Arena, Melbourne, Australia
27th April	Rod Laver Arena, Melbourne, Australia
28th April	Rod Laver Arena, Melbourne, Australia
30th April	Sydney Entertainment Centre, Sydney, Australia
1st May	Sydney Entertainment Centre, Sydney, Australia
4th May	Brisbane Entertainment Centre, Brisbane, Australia
5th May	Brisbane Entertainment Centre, Brisbane, Australia
6th May	GCCEC Arena, Gold Coast, Australia
8th May	Newcastle Entertainment Centre, Newcastle, Australia
9th May	Newcastle Entertainment Centre, Newcastle, Australia
11th May	Sydney Entertainment Centre, Sydney, Australia
12th May	Sydney Entertainment Centre, Sydney, Australia
13th May	Sydney Entertainment Centre, Sydney, Australia
15th May	Rod Laver Arena, Melbourne, Australia
16th May	Rod Laver Arena, Melbourne, Australia
17th May	Adelaide Entertainment Centre, Adelaide, Australia
19th May	AIS Arena, Canberra, Australia
20th May	AIS Arena, Canberra, Australia
21st May	Newcastle Entertainment Centre, Newcastle, Australia
23rd May	WIN Entertainment Centre, Wollongong, Australia
25th May	Brisbane Entertainment Centre, Brisbane, Australia
26th May	Brisbane Entertainment Centre, Brisbane, Australia
28th May	Sydney Entertainment Centre, Sydney, Australia
29th May	Rod Laver Arena, Melbourne, Australia
30th May	Adelaide Entertainment Centre, Adelaide, Australia
2nd June	Challenge Stadium, Perth, Australia
3rd June	Challenge Stadium, Perth, Australia
4th June	Challenge Stadium, Perth, Australia
7th June	Sydney Entertainment Centre, Sydney, Australia
8th June	Brisbane Entertainment Centre, Brisbane, Australia
10th June	Vector Arena, Auckland, New Zealand

23rd June	Malahide Castle, Malahide, Ireland
26th June	Trädgår'n, Gothenburg, Sweden
28th June	Skopje City Stadium, Skopje, F.Y.R. Macedonia
30th June	Romexpo, Bucharest, Romania
5th July	Tivoli Hall, Ljubljana, Slovenia
6th July	Burg Clam, Klam, Austria
7th July	Werchter Festival Grounds, Werchter, Belgium
11th July	Möslestadion, Götzis, Austria
12th July	Moon and Stars Festival, Locarno, Switzerland
15th July	Edinburgh Castle Esplanade, Edinburgh, Scotland
16th July	Liverpool Summer Pops, Liverpool, England
18th July	Marktplatz Lörrach, Lörrach, Germany
21st July	Heide Park Eventfläche, Soltau, Germany
22nd July	Stadthaus Ulm, Ulm, Germany
25th July	Cavea Auditorium, Rome, Italy
26th July	Paléo Festival, Nyon, Switzerland
28th July	Ehrenhof, Mannheim, Germany
29th July	Festplatz Teisnach, Teisnach, Germany
30th July	Stadthalle Graz, Graz, Austria
3rd August	Sportplatz Oberstadt, Imst, Austria
8th August	Lokerse Feesten, Lokeren, Belgium
10th August	Óbudai-sziget, Sziget Festival, Hungary
11th August	Heiternplatz, Zofingen, Switzerland
12th August	Taubertal Festival, Rothenburg, Germany
14th August	Brixton Academy, London, England
15th August	Brixton Academy, London, England
17th August	Veste Coburg Square, Coburg, Germany
18th August	Hylands Park, Chelmsford, England
19th August	Hylands Park, Stafford, England
22nd August	Plymouth Pavilions, Plymouth, England
23rd August	Brighton Centre, Brighton, England
25th August	Gerry Weber Stadion, Halle, Germany
26th August	AmphiTheatre Gelsenkirchen, Gelsenkirchen, Germany
28th August	Odense Cattle Showgrounds, Odense, Denmark
30th August	Sommergarten, Berlin, Germany
1st September	Beatstad Malieveld, The Hague, Netherlands
5th September	Dubai Media City Amphitheatre, Dubai, United Arab Emirates
8th September	Super Bowl Arena, North West, South Africa
9th September	Coca-Cola Dome, Johannesburg, South Africa
11th September	Bellville Velodrome, Cape Town, South Africa

Funhouse Tour 2009

24th February	Palais Nikaïa, Nice, France
26th February	Sportpaleis, Antwerp, Belgium
28th February	Sportpaleis van Ahoy, Rotterdam, Netherlands
1st March	Sportpaleis van Ahoy, Rotterdam, Netherlands
5th March	Donau Arena, Regensburg, Germany
6th March	Messe Friedrichshafen, Friedrichshafen, Germany
8th March	König Pilsener Arena, Oberhausen, Germany
9th March	Palais Omnisports de Paris-Bercy, Paris, France
12th March	SAP Arena, Mannheim, Germany
14th March	Hanns-Martin-Schleyer-Halle, Stuttgart, Germany
17th March	Arena Leipzig, Leipzig, Germany
18th March	O2 World, Berlin, Germany
21st March	SEG Geneva Arena, Geneva, Switzerland
22nd March	Hallenstadion, Zürich, Switzerland
24th March	Budapest Sports Arena, Budapest, Hungary
25th March	Wiener Stadthalle, Vienna, Austria
27th March	Festhalle Frankfurt, Frankfurt, Germany
28th March	Arena Nürnberger Versicherung, Nuremberg, Germany
30th March	Lanxess Arena, Cologne, Germany
1st April	Color Line Arena, Hamburg, Germany

Gigography

2nd April	Color Line Arena, Hamburg, Germany
4th April	TUI Arena, Hanover, Germany
6th April	Olympiahalle, Munich, Germany
7th April	Olympiahalle, Munich, Germany
8th April	Westfalenhallen, Dortmund, Germany
11th April	Scottish Exhibition Centre, Hall 4, Glasgow, Scotland
12th April	Scottish Exhibition Centre, Hall 4, Glasgow, Scotland
13th April	Press & Journal Arena, Aberdeen, Scotland
16th April	National Indoor Arena, Birmingham, England
17th April	National Indoor Arena, Birmingham, England
19th April	The O2, Dublin, Ireland
20th April	The O2, Dublin, Ireland
22nd April	Odyssey Arena, Belfast, Northern Ireland
23rd April	Odyssey Arena, Belfast, Northern Ireland
25th April	Manchester Evening News Arena, Manchester, England
26th April	Manchester Evening News Arena, Manchester, England
28th April	Metro Radio Arena, Newcastle, England
29th April	Echo Arena Liverpool, Liverpool, England
1st May	The O2 Arena, London, England
2nd May	The O2 Arena, London, England
4th May	The O2 Arena, London, England
22nd May	Burswood Dome, Perth, Australia
23rd May	Burswood Dome, Perth, Australia
26th May	Adelaide Entertainment Centre, Adelaide, Australia
27th May	Adelaide Entertainment Centre, Adelaide, Australia
30th May	Rod Laver Arena, Melbourne, Australia
31st May	Rod Laver Arena, Melbourne, Australia
3rd June	Newcastle Entertainment Centre, Newcastle, Australia
4th June	Newcastle Entertainment Centre, Newcastle, Australia
6th June	Sydney Entertainment Centre, Sydney, Australia
7th June	Sydney Entertainment Centre, Sydney, Australia
9th June	Sydney Entertainment Centre, Sydney, Australia
10th June	Sydney Entertainment Centre, Sydney, Australia
12th June	Brisbane Entertainment Centre, Brisbane, Australia
13th June	Brisbane Entertainment Centre, Brisbane, Australia
15th June	Brisbane Entertainment Centre, Brisbane, Australia
16th June	Brisbane Entertainment Centre, Brisbane, Australia
18th June	Rod Laver Arena, Melbourne, Australia
20th June	Rod Laver Arena, Melbourne, Australia
21st June	Rod Laver Arena, Melbourne, Australia
23rd June	Rod Laver Arena, Melbourne, Australia
24th June	Rod Laver Arena, Melbourne, Australia
26th June	Sydney Entertainment Centre, Sydney, Australia
27th June	Sydney Entertainment Centre, Sydney, Australia
29th June	Sydney Entertainment Centre, Sydney, Australia
30th June	Sydney Entertainment Centre, Sydney, Australia
3rd July	Newcastle Entertainment Centre, Newcastle, Australia
4th July	Newcastle Entertainment Centre, Newcastle, Australia
14th July	Rod Laver Arena, Melbourne, Australia
15th July	Rod Laver Arena, Melbourne, Australia
17th July	Sydney Entertainment Centre, Sydney, Australia
18th July	Sydney Entertainment Centre, Sydney, Australia
22nd July	Brisbane Entertainment Centre, Brisbane, Australia
23rd July	Brisbane Entertainment Centre, Brisbane, Australia
25th July	Brisbane Entertainment Centre, Brisbane, Australia
26th July	Brisbane Entertainment Centre, Brisbane, Australia
27th July	Brisbane Entertainment Centre, Brisbane, Australia
29th July	Rod Laver Arena, Melbourne, Australia
30th July	Rod Laver Arena, Melbourne, Australia
1st August	Rod Laver Arena, Melbourne, Australia
2nd August	Rod Laver Arena, Melbourne, Australia
4th August	Adelaide Entertainment Centre, Adelaide, Australia
5th August	Adelaide Entertainment Centre, Adelaide, Australia
7th August	Burswood Dome, Perth, Australia
8th August	Burswood Dome, Perth, Australia

10th August	Adelaide Entertainment Centre, Adelaide, Australia
11th August	Adelaide Entertainment Centre, Adelaide, Australia
13th August	Rod Laver Arena, Melbourne, Australia
14th August	Rod Laver Arena, Melbourne, Australia
16th August	AIS Arena, Canberra, Australia
17th August	AIS Arena, Canberra, Australia
19th August	Rod Laver Arena, Melbourne, Australia
20th August	Rod Laver Arena, Melbourne, Australia
22nd August	WIN Entertainment Centre, Wollongong, Australia
23rd August	WIN Entertainment Centre, Wollongong, Australia
25th August	Brisbane Entertainment Centre, Brisbane, Australia
26th August	Brisbane Entertainment Centre, Brisbane, Australia
28th August	Acer Arena, Sydney, Australia
29th August	Acer Arena, Sydney, Australia
15th September	KeyArena, Seattle, US
17th September	HP Pavilion, San Jose, US
18th September	Staples Centre, Los Angeles, US
20th September	Jobing.com Arena, Glendale, US
23rd September	American Airlines Centre, Dallas, US
24th September	Toyota Centre, Houston, US
26th September	Allstate Arena, Rosemont, US
28th September	Patriot Centre, Fairfax, US
30th September	Air Canada Centre, Toronto, Canada
2nd October	TD Garden, Boston, US
3rd October	Wachovia Spectrum, Philadelphia, US
5th October	Madison Square Garden, New York City, US
14th October	The O2, Dublin, Ireland
15th October	The O2, Dublin, Ireland
17th October	Odyssey Arena, Belfast, Northern Ireland
18th October	Odyssey Arena, Belfast, Northern Ireland
20th October	Scottish Exhibition Centre, Hall 4, Glasgow, Scotland
21st October	Scottish Exhibition Centre, Hall 4, Glasgow, Scotland
23rd October	Manchester Evening News Arena, Manchester, England
24th October	Manchester Evening News Arena, Manchester, England
25th October	Manchester Evening News Arena, Manchester, England
27th October	Echo Arena, Liverpool, England
28th October	Sheffield Arena, Sheffield, England
30th October	National Indoor Arena, Birmingham, England
31st October	National Indoor Arena, Birmingham, England
2nd November	Metro Radio Arena, Newcastle, England
3rd November	Trent FM Arena, Nottingham, England
5th November	Sportpaleis, Antwerp, Belgium
7th November	Forum Copenhagen, Copenhagen, Denmark
9th November	Oslo Spektrum, Oslo, Norway
10th November	Ericsson Globe, Stockholm, Sweden
12th November	Hartwall Areena, Helsinki, Finland
19th November	O2 Arena, Prague, Czech Republic
20th November	Frankfurt Festhalle, Frankfurt, Germany
21st November	Olympiahalle, Munich, Germany
23rd November	Messe Freiburg, Freiburg, Germany
25th November	Hanns-Martin-Schleyer-Halle, Stuttgart, Germany
26th November	Messe Erfurt, Erfurt, Germany
28th November	ISS Dome, Düsseldorf, Germany
30th November	König Pilsener Arena, Oberhausen, Germany
2nd December	Hallenstadion, Zürich, Switzerland
3rd December	Hallenstadion, Zürich, Switzerland
5th December	Rockhal, Esch-sur-Alzette, Luxembourg
6th December	Rotterdam Ahoy, Rotterdam, Netherlands
8th December	The O2 Arena, London, England
10th December	The O2 Arena, London, England
12th December	AWD Dome, Bremen, Germany
13th December	Westfalenhallen, Dortmund, Germany
15th December	SEG Geneva Arena, Geneva, Switzerland
17th December	Wiener Stadthalle, Vienna, Austria
19th December	Hanns-Martin-Schleyer-Halle, Stuttgart, Germany
20th December	TUI Arena, Hanover, Germany

The Funhouse Summer Carnival Tour 2010

29th May	RheinEnergieStadion, Cologne, Germany
30th May	Megaland Landgraaf, Landgraaf, Netherlands
2nd June	Frankenstadion, Heilbronn, Germany
3rd June	Hessentagsarena Open Air Gelände, Stadtallendorf, Germany
5th June	Außenanlagen, Innsbruck, Austria
6th June	Olympia Reitstadion Riem, Munich, Germany
8th June	Waldbühne, Berlin, Germany
11th June	Stadium of Light, Sunderland, England
12th June	Reebok Stadium, Bolton, England
13th June	Seaclose Park, Newport, England
16th June	King's Hall Complex Grounds, Belfast, Northern Ireland
19th June	RDS Arena, Dublin, Ireland
20th June	Thomond Park, Limerick, Ireland
23rd June	Liberty Stadium, Swansea, Wales
24th June	Ricoh Arena, Coventry, England
26th June	Hampden Park, Glasgow, Scotland
27th June	Alton Towers, Alton, England
29th June	Portman Road, Ipswich, England
2nd July	Hyde Park, London, England
3rd July	Werchter Festival Grounds, Werchter, Belgium
4th July	Citadelle d'Arras, Arras, France
6th July	Arena of Nîmes, Nîmes, France
8th July	Linzer Stadion, Linz, Austria
10th July	Stade de Suisse, Bern, Switzerland
12th July	Piazza Grande, Locarno, Switzerland
13th July	Stade Charles-Ehrmann, Nice, France
15th July	EasyCredit-Stadion, Nuremberg, Germany
16th July	Schule Schloss Salem, Salem, Germany
18th July	Saint Petersburg TV Tower, Saint Petersburg, Russia
20th July	Synot Tip Arena, Prague, Czech Republic
21st July	Kaisaniemi Park, Helsinki, Finland
23rd July	Ullevi Stadium, Gothenburg, Sweden
24th July	Parken Stadium, Copenhagen, Denmark
25th July	Odderøya Amfi, Kristiansand, Norway

The Truth About Love Tour 2013

13th February	US Airways Centre, Phoenix, US
15th February	Mandalay Bay Events Centre, Las Vegas, US
16th February	Staples Centre, Los Angeles, US
18th February	HP Pavilion, San Jose, US
21st February	Toyota Centre, Houston, US
22nd February	American Airlines Centre, Dallas, US
24th February	Amway Centre, Orlando, US
25th February	BB&T Centre, Sunrise, US
27th February	Tampa Bay Times Forum, Tampa, US
1st March	Philips Arena, Atlanta, US
2nd March	Bridgestone Arena, Nashville, US
5th March	The Palace of Auburn Hills, Auburn Hills, US
6th March	Schottenstein Centre, Columbus, US
8th March	KFC Yum! Centre, Louisville, US
9th March	United Centre, Chicago, US
11th March	Air Canada Centre, Toronto, Canada
12th March	Bell Centre, Montreal, Canada
14th March	Verizon Centre, Washington, D.C., US
16th March	Time Warner Cable Arena, Charlotte, US
17th March	Wells Fargo Centre, Philadelphia, US
19th March	Xcel Energy Centre, Saint Paul, US
22nd March	Madison Square Garden, New York City, US
23rd March	Izod Centre, East Rutherford, US
25th March	Nassau Coliseum, Uniondale, US

Glitter in the Air - *The Evolution of Pink*

27th March	Mohegan Sun Arena, Uncasville, US
28th March	TD Garden, Boston, US
12th April	The O2, Dublin, Ireland
14th April	Phones 4u Arena, Manchester, England
15th April	Phones 4u Arena, Manchester, England
17th April	Palais Omnisports de Paris-Bercy, Paris, France
19th April	Ziggo Dome, Amsterdam, Netherlands
21st April	National Indoor Arena, Birmingham, England
24th April	The O2 Arena, London, England
25th April	The O2 Arena, London, England
27th April	The O2 Arena, London, England
28th April	The O2 Arena, London, England
30th April	Sportpaleis, Antwerp, Belgium
1st May	O2 World Hamburg, Hamburg, Germany
3rd May	O2 World, Berlin, Germany
4th May	TUI Arena, Hanover, Germany
6th May	ISS Dome, Düsseldorf, Germany
7th May	Festhalle, Frankfurt, Germany
9th May	Wiener Stadthalle, Vienna, Austria
10th May	O2 Arena, Prague, Czech Republic
12th May	Arena Leipzig, Leipzig, Germany
13th May	Westfalenhalle, Dortmund, Germany
15th May	König-Pilsener-Arena, Oberhausen, Germany
16th May	SAP Arena, Mannheim, Germany
18th May	Olympiahalle, Munich, Germany
19th May	Olympiahalle, Munich, Germany
21st May	Hallenstadion, Zürich, Switzerland
22nd May	Hanns-Martin-Schleyer-Halle, Stuttgart, Germany
25th May	Telenor Arena, Oslo, Norway
26th May	Ericsson Globe, Stockholm, Sweden
28th May	Hartwall Arena, Helsinki, Finland
30th May	Jyske Bank Boxen, Herning, Denmark
25th June	Perth Arena, Perth, Australia
26th June	Perth Arena, Perth, Australia
28th June	Perth Arena, Perth, Australia
29th June	Perth Arena, Perth, Australia
1st July	Entertainment Centre Arena, Adelaide, Australia
2nd July	Entertainment Centre Arena, Adelaide, Australia
4th July	Entertainment Centre Arena, Adelaide, Australia
5th July	Entertainment Centre Arena, Adelaide, Australia
7th July	Rod Laver Arena, Melbourne, Australia
8th July	Rod Laver Arena, Melbourne, Australia
10th July	Rod Laver Arena, Melbourne, Australia
11th July	Rod Laver Arena, Melbourne, Australia
13th July	Rod Laver Arena, Melbourne, Australia
14th July	Rod Laver Arena, Melbourne, Australia
16th July	Rod Laver Arena, Melbourne, Australia
17th July	Rod Laver Arena, Melbourne, Australia
19th July	Brisbane Entertainment Centre, Brisbane, Australia
20th July	Brisbane Entertainment Centre, Brisbane, Australia
22nd July	Brisbane Entertainment Centre, Brisbane, Australia
23rd July	Brisbane Entertainment Centre, Brisbane, Australia
30th July	Sydney Entertainment Centre, Sydney, Australia
31st July	Sydney Entertainment Centre, Sydney, Australia
2nd August	Sydney Entertainment Centre, Sydney, Australia
3rd August	Sydney Entertainment Centre, Sydney, Australia
6th August	Sydney Entertainment Centre, Sydney, Australia
7th August	Sydney Entertainment Centre, Sydney, Australia
9th August	Sydney Entertainment Centre, Sydney, Australia
10th August	Sydney Entertainment Centre, Sydney, Australia
13th August	Rod Laver Arena, Melbourne, Australia
14th August	Rod Laver Arena, Melbourne, Australia
16th August	Rod Laver Arena, Melbourne, Australia
17th August	Rod Laver Arena, Melbourne, Australia
19th August	Rod Laver Arena, Melbourne, Australia

20th August	Rod Laver Arena, Melbourne, Australia
22nd August	Rod Laver Arena, Melbourne, Australia
23rd August	Rod Laver Arena, Melbourne, Australia
25th August	Rod Laver Arena, Melbourne, Australia
26th August	Rod Laver Arena, Melbourne, Australia
29th August	Brisbane Entertainment Centre, Brisbane, Australia
30th August	Brisbane Entertainment Centre, Brisbane, Australia
1st September	Allphones Arena, Sydney, Australia
2nd September	Allphones Arena, Sydney, Australia
4th September	Allphones Arena, Sydney, Australia
5th September	Allphones Arena, Sydney, Australia
7th September	Brisbane Entertainment Centre, Brisbane, Australia
8th September	Brisbane Entertainment Centre, Brisbane, Australia
10th October	Oracle Arena, Oakland, US
12th October	Staples Centre, Los Angeles, US
13th October	Staples Centre, Los Angeles, US
15th October	SAP Centre, San Jose, US
20th October	KeyArena, Seattle, US
21st October	Rogers Arena, Vancouver, Canada
5th November	United Centre, Chicago, US
6th November	The Palace of Auburn Hills, Auburn Hills, US
8th November	Wells Fargo Arena, Des Moines, US
9th November	Pinnacle Bank Arena, Lincoln, US
11th November	Scottrade Centre, St. Louis, US
12th November	Sprint Centre, Kansas City, US
14th November	AT&T Centre, San Antonio, US
16th November	American Airlines Centre, Dallas, US
17th November	Verizon Arena, North Little Rock, US
20th November	Allstate Arena, Rosemont, US
21st November	Bankers Life Fieldhouse, Indianapolis, US
23rd November	Quicken Loans Arena, Cleveland, US
24th November	Verizon Centre, Washington, D.C., US
30th November	Air Canada Centre, Toronto, Canada
2nd December	Air Canada Centre, Toronto, Canada
3rd December	Bell Centre, Montreal, Canada
5th December	TD Garden, Boston, US
6th December	Wells Fargo Centre, Philadelphia, US
8th December	Barclays Centre, Brooklyn, US
9th December	Barclays Centre, Brooklyn, US
11th December	Prudential Centre, Newark, US
13th December	BJCC Arena, Birmingham, US
14th December	Philips Arena, Atlanta, US

The Truth About Love Tour 2014

7th January	Target Centre, Minneapolis, US
9th January	BMO Harris Bradley Centre, Milwaukee, US
11th January	Fargodome, Fargo, US
14th January	MTS Centre, Winnipeg, Canada
15th January	Credit Union Centre, Saskatoon, Canada
16th January	Rexall Place, Edmonton, Canada
19th January	Pepsi Centre, Denver, US
20th January	EnergySolutions Arena, Salt Lake City, US
29th January	Honda Centre, Anaheim, US
30th January	Save Mart Centre, Fresno, US
31st January	MGM Grand Garden Arena, Las Vegas, US

Beautiful Trauma World Tour 2018

1st March	Talking Stick Resort Arena, Phoenix, US
3rd March	Intrust Bank Arena, Wichita, US
5th March	BOK Centre, Tulsa, US

Glitter in the Air - *The Evolution of Pink*

6th March	Pinnacle Bank Arena, Lincoln, US
9th March	United Centre, Chicago, US
10th March	United Centre, Chicago, US
12th March	Xcel Energy Centre, Saint Paul, US
14th March	Scottrade Centre, St. Louis, US
15th March	Sprint Centre, Kansas City, US
17th March	Bankers Life Fieldhouse, Indianapolis, US
18th March	Van Andel Arena, Grand Rapids, US
20th March	Air Canada Centre, Toronto, Canada
21st March	Air Canada Centre, Toronto, Canada
27th March	KFC Yum! Centre, Louisville, US
28th March	Quicken Loans Arena, Cleveland, US
4th April	Madison Square Garden, New York City, US
5th April	Madison Square Garden, New York City, US
7th April	PPG Paints Arena, Pittsburgh, US
9th April	TD Garden, Boston, US
10th April	TD Garden, Boston, US
13th April	Wells Fargo Centre, Philadelphia, US
14th April	Prudential Centre, Newark, US
16th April	Capital One Arena, Washington, D.C., US
17th April	Capital One Arena, Washington, D.C., US
19th April	John Paul Jones Arena, Charlottesville, US
21st April	Philips Arena, Atlanta, US
24th April	Amway Centre, Orlando, US
25th April	BB&T Centre, Sunrise, US
27th April	Toyota Centre, Houston, US
28th April	Toyota Centre, Houston, US
1st May	American Airlines Centre, Dallas, US
2nd May	American Airlines Centre, Dallas, US
8th May	Pepsi Centre, Denver, US
9th May	Vivint Smart Home Arena, Salt Lake City, US
12th May	Rogers Arena, Vancouver, Canada
13th May	KeyArena, Seattle, US
15th May	Moda Centre, Portland, US
18th May	Oracle Arena, Oakland, US
19th May	Oracle Arena, Oakland, US
22nd May	Save Mart Centre, Fresno, US
23rd May	Citizens Business Bank Arena, Ontario, US
25th May	Honda Centre, Anaheim, US
26th May	T-Mobile Arena, Las Vegas, US
28th May	Valley View Casino Centre, San Diego, US
31st May	Staples Centre, Los Angeles, US
1st June	The Forum, Inglewood, US
3rd July	RAC Arena, Perth, Australia
4th July	RAC Arena, Perth, Australia
6th July	RAC Arena, Perth, Australia
7th July	RAC Arena, Perth, Australia
10th July	Entertainment Centre Arena, Adelaide, Australia
11th July	Entertainment Centre Arena, Adelaide, Australia
13th July	Entertainment Centre Arena, Adelaide, Australia
14th July	Entertainment Centre Arena, Adelaide, Australia
16th July	Rod Laver Arena, Melbourne, Australia
17th July	Rod Laver Arena, Melbourne, Australia
19th July	Rod Laver Arena, Melbourne, Australia
20th July	Rod Laver Arena, Melbourne, Australia
22nd July	Rod Laver Arena, Melbourne, Australia
23rd July	Rod Laver Arena, Melbourne, Australia
25th July	Rod Laver Arena, Melbourne, Australia
27th July	Rod Laver Arena, Melbourne, Australia
28th July	Rod Laver Arena, Melbourne, Australia
4th August	Qudos Bank Arena, Sydney, Australia
11th August	Qudos Bank Arena, Sydney, Australia
12th August	Qudos Bank Arena, Sydney, Australia
14th August	Brisbane Entertainment Centre, Brisbane, Australia
15th August	Brisbane Entertainment Centre, Brisbane, Australia

17th August	Brisbane Entertainment Centre, Brisbane, Australia
18th August	Brisbane Entertainment Centre, Brisbane, Australia
20th August	Brisbane Entertainment Centre, Brisbane, Australia
21st August	Brisbane Entertainment Centre, Brisbane, Australia
22nd August	Brisbane Entertainment Centre, Brisbane, Australia
24th August	Qudos Bank Arena, Sydney, Australia
25th August	Qudos Bank Arena, Sydney, Australia
26th August	Qudos Bank Arena, Sydney, Australia
28th August	Rod Laver Arena, Melbourne, Australia
29th August	Rod Laver Arena, Melbourne, Australia
1st September	Forsyth Barr Stadium, Dunedin, New Zealand
4th September	Spark Arena, Auckland, New Zealand
5th September	Spark Arena, Auckland, New Zealand
7th September	Spark Arena, Auckland, New Zealand
8th September	Spark Arena, Auckland, New Zealand
10th September	Spark Arena, Auckland, New Zealand
11th September	Spark Arena, Auckland, New Zealand
17th September	Qudos Bank Arena, Sydney, Australia
18th September	Qudos Bank Arena, Sydney, Australia
19th September	Qudos Bank Arena, Sydney, Australia

Beautiful Trauma World Tour 2019

1st March	BB&T Centre, Sunrise, US
3rd March	Amalie Arena, Tampa, US
5th March	Jacksonville Veterans Memorial Arena, Jacksonville, US
7th March	Colonial Life Arena, Columbia, US
9th March	Spectrum Centre, Charlotte, US
10th March	Bridgestone Arena, Nashville, US
12th March	State Farm Arena, Atlanta, US
14th March	Legacy Arena, Birmingham, US
16th March	CenturyLink Centre, Bossier City, US
17th March	Smoothie King Centre, New Orleans, US
19th March	Toyota Centre, Houston, US
21st March	AT&T Centre, San Antonio, US
23rd March	Chesapeake Energy Arena, Oklahoma City, US
24th March	American Airlines Centre, Dallas, US
30th March	Gila River Arena, Glendale, US
1st April	Pepsi Centre, Denver, US
3rd April	Vivint Smart Home Arena, Salt Lake City, US
5th April	Rogers Arena, Vancouver, Canada
6th April	Rogers Arena, Vancouver, Canada
8th April	Moda Centre, Portland, US
10th April	Golden 1 Centre, Sacramento, US
12th April	T-Mobile Arena, Las Vegas, US
13th April	Honda Centre, Anaheim, US
15th April	Staples Centre, Los Angeles, US
17th April	SAP Centre, San Jose, US
19th April	The Forum, Inglewood, US
26th April	Little Caesars Arena, Detroit, US
27th April	Little Caesars Arena, Detroit, US
30th April	Bankers Life Fieldhouse, Indianapolis, US
2nd May	Fiserv Forum, Milwaukee, US
4th May	Fargodome, Fargo, US
5th May	Xcel Energy Centre, Saint Paul, US
7th May	CHI Health Centre Omaha, Omaha, US
9th May	Rupp Arena, Lexington, US
11th May	Schottenstein Centre, Columbus, US
17th May	Bell Centre, Montreal, Canada
18th May	Bell Centre, Montreal, Canada
21st May	Madison Square Garden, New York City, US
22nd May	Madison Square Garden, New York City, US
16th June	Johan Cruyff Arena, Amsterdam, Netherlands

18th June	RDS Arena, Dublin, Ireland
20th June	Principality Stadium, Cardiff, Wales
22nd June	Hampden Park, Glasgow, Scotland
23rd June	Hampden Park, Glasgow, Scotland
25th June	Anfield Stadium, Liverpool, England
27th June	Werchter Festival Park, Werchter, Belgium
29th June	Wembley Stadium, London, England
30th June	Wembley Stadium, London, England
3rd July	Paris La Défense Arena, Nanterre, France
5th July	RheinEnergieStadion, Cologne, Germany
6th July	RheinEnergieStadion, Cologne, Germany
8th July	Volksparkstadion, Hamburg, Germany
10th July	Mercedes-Benz Arena, Stuttgart, Germany
12th July	HDI-Arena, Hanover, Germany
14th July	Olympiastadion, Berlin, Germany
20th July	PGE Narodowy, Warsaw, Poland
22nd July	Commerzbank-Arena, Frankfurt, Germany
24th July	Ernst-Happel-Stadion, Vienna, Austria
26th July	Olympiastadion, Munich, Germany
27th July	Olympiastadion, Munich, Germany
30th July	Letzigrund, Zürich, Switzerland
3rd August	Tele2 Arena, Stockholm, Sweden
5th August	Telenor Arena, Oslo, Norway
7th August	CASA Arena Horsens, Horsens, Denmark
9th August	Veltins-Arena, Gelsenkirchen, Germany
11th August	Malieveld, The Hague, Netherlands
16th August	Nassau Coliseum, Uniondale, US
18th August	Scotiabank Arena, Toronto, Canada
19th August	Scotiabank Arena, Toronto, Canada
5th October	Barra Olympic Park, Rio de Janeiro, Brazil
2nd November	Circuit of the Americas, Austin, US

Summer Carnival Tour 2023

7th June	University of Bolton Stadium, Bolton, England
8th June	University of Bolton Stadium, Bolton, England
10th June	Stadium of Light, Sunderland, England
11th June	Stadium of Light, Sunderland, England
13th June	Villa Park, Birmingham, England
16th June	Megaland Park, Landgraaf, Netherlands
17th June	Festivalpark Werchter, Werchter, Belgium
20th June	La Défense Arena, Nanterre, France
21st June	La Défense Arena, Nanterre, France
24th June	Hyde Park, London, England
25th June	Hyde Park, London, England
28th June	Olympiastadion, Berlin, Germany
1st July	Ernst-Happel-Stadion, Vienna, Austria
2nd July	Ernst-Happel-Stadion, Vienna, Austria
5th July	Olympiastadion, Munich, Germany
6th July	Olympiastadion, Munich, Germany
8th July	RheinEnergieStadion, Cologne, Germany
9th July	RheinEnergieStadion, Cologne, Germany
12th July	HDI-Arena, Hanover, Germany
13th July	HDI-Arena, Hanover, Germany
16th July	PGE Narodowy, Warsaw, Poland
24th July	Rogers Centre, Toronto, Canada
26th July	Great American Ball Park, Cincinnati, US
31st July	Fenway Park, Boston, US
1st August	Fenway Park, Boston, US
3rd August	Citi Field, New York City, US
5th August	PNC Park, Pittsburgh, US
7th August	Nationals Park, Washington, D.C.
10th August	Target Field, Minneapolis, US

12th August	Wrigley Field, Chicago, US
14th August	American Family Field, Milwaukee, US
16th August	Comerica Park, Detroit, US
19th August	Fargodome, Fargo, US
21st August	Charles Schwab Field Omaha, Omaha, US
15th September	Piedmont Park, Atlanta, US
18th September	Citizens Bank Park, Philadelphia, US
19th September	Citizens Bank Park, Philadelphia, US
22nd September	Geodis Park, Nashville, US
25th September	Alamodome, San Antonio, US
27th September	Minute Maid Park, Houston, US
3rd October	Snapdragon Stadium, San Diego, US
5th October	SoFi Stadium, Inglewood, US
7th October	Allegiant Stadium, Paradise, US
9th October	Chase Field, Phoenix, US

Trustfall Tour 2023

12th October	Chase Centre, San Francisco, US
15th October	Chase Centre, San Francisco, US
25th October	Ball Arena, Denver, US
27th October	T-Mobile Centre, Kansas City, US
28th October	T-Mobile Centre, Kansas City, US
1st November	Bell Centre, Montreal, Canada
2nd November	Bell Centre, Montreal, Canada
4th November	Madison Square Garden, New York City, US
5th November	Madison Square Garden, New York City, US
7th November	Gainbridge Fieldhouse, Indianapolis, US
8th November	Rocket Mortgage FieldHouse, Cleveland, US
11th November	KFC Yum! Centre, Louisville, US
12th November	Spectrum Centre, Charlotte, US
14th November	Kaseya Centre, Miami, US
15th November	Amerant Bank Arena, Sunrise, US
18th November	Amway Centre, Orlando, US
19th November	Amway Centre, Orlando, US

Summer Carnival Tour 2024

9th February	Allianz Stadium, Sydney, Australia
10th February	Allianz Stadium, Sydney, Australia
13th February	McDonald Jones Stadium, Newcastle, Australia
16th February	Suncorp Stadium, Brisbane, Australia
17th February	Suncorp Stadium, Brisbane, Australia
20th February	Heritage Bank Stadium, Gold Coast, Australia
23rd February	Marvel Stadium, Melbourne, Australia
24th February	Marvel Stadium, Melbourne, Australia
27th February	Adelaide Oval, Adelaide, Australia
1st March	Optus Stadium, Perth, Australia
2nd March	Optus Stadium, Perth, Australia
5th March	Forsyth Barr Stadium, Dunedin, New Zealand
8th March	Eden Park, Auckland, New Zealand
9th March	Eden Park, Auckland, New Zealand
12th March	Marvel Stadium, Melbourne, Australia
13th March	Marvel Stadium, Melbourne, Australia
16th March	Accor Stadium, Sydney, Australia
19th March	Suncorp Stadium, Brisbane, Australia
22nd March	Queensland Country Bank Stadium, Townsville, Australia
23rd March	Queensland Country Bank Stadium, Townsville, Australia
11th June	Principality Stadium, Cardiff, Wales
15th June	Tottenham Hotspur Stadium, London, England
16th June	Tottenham Hotspur Stadium, London, England
20th June	Aviva Stadium, Dublin, Ireland

21st June	Aviva Stadium, Dublin, Ireland
24th June	Anfield, Liverpool, England
25th June	Anfield, Liverpool, England
28th June	Hampden Park, Glasgow, Scotland
29th June	Hampden Park, Glasgow, Scotland
6th July	Parken Stadium, Copenhagen, Denmark
10th July	Johan Cruijff Arena, Amsterdam, Netherlands
11th July	Johan Cruijff Arena, Amsterdam, Netherlands
14th July	King Baudouin Stadium, Brussels, Belgium
17th July	Red Bull Arena, Leipzig, Germany
19th July	MHPArena, Stuttgart, Germany
21st July	Borussia-Park, Mönchengladbach, Germany
25th July	Friends Arena, Stockholm, Sweden
10th August	The Dome at America's Centre, St. Louis, US
14th August	Rogers Centre, Toronto, Canada
18th August	Lincoln Financial Field, Philadelphia, US
21st August	Gillette Stadium, Foxborough, US
24th August	Soldier Field, Chicago, US
28th August	Washington–Grizzly Stadium, Missoula, US
31st August	Commonwealth Stadium, Edmonton, Canada

Trustfall Tour 2024

3rd September	Tacoma Dome, Tacoma, US
4th September	Tacoma Dome, Tacoma, US
6th September	Rogers Arena, Vancouver, Canada
7th September	Rogers Arena, Vancouver, Canada

Summer Carnival Tour 2024

11th September	Petco Park, San Diego, US
13th September	Allegiant Stadium, Paradise, US
15th September	Dodger Stadium, Los Angeles, US
1st October	Hersheypark Stadium, Hershey, US
3rd October	MetLife Stadium, East Rutherford, US
6th October	JMA Wireless Dome, Syracuse, US

Trustfall Tour 2004

9th October	Value City Arena, Columbus, US

Summer Carnival Tour 2024

12th October	Lucas Oil Stadium, Indianapolis, US

Trustfall Tour 2024

14th October	Little Caesars Arena, Detroit, US
15th October	Little Caesars Arena, Detroit, US
17th October	Xcel Energy Centre, Saint Paul, US
18th October	Xcel Energy Centre, Saint Paul, US
3rd November	Moody Centre, Austin, US

Summer Carnival Tour 2024

6th November	Globe Life Field, Arlington, US

Trustfall Tour 2024

8th November BOK Centre, Tulsa, US
11th November PNC Arena, Raleigh, US
12th November PNC Arena, Raleigh, US
14th November State Farm Arena, Atlanta, US
16th November Legacy Arena, Birmingham, US

Summer Carnival Tour 2024

18th November Camping World Stadium, Orlando, US

Trustfall Tour 2024

20th November Colonial Life Arena, Columbia, US

About The Author

As an author, Laura Shenton is probably best known for her music non-fiction. In particular, *Dance With The Devil – The Cozy Powell Story* (Wymer Publishing) and *Tommy Bolin – In and Out of Deep Purple* (Sonicbond Publishing). She feels that preserving the legacies of musicians who have contributed something amazing to the field is imperative.

For readers who want to enjoy the ride of letting their mind get lost in a good story without having to commit to a lengthy read, then it might just be that Laura's fiction books could be your cup of tea. They are character-driven with a short and punchy narrative that gets to the point. They are all novellas or novelettes. Genres include gothic, fantasy, and adventure (mostly, but with a few diversions too).

And finally, Laura's children's books… They are simple, accessible and fun. A good choice for youngsters with a fertile imagination who are at the very start of their reading journey.